Writing *for IELTS*

with Answer Key

4.5–6.0

Sam McCarter • Norman Whitby

MACMILLAN

Macmillan Education
4 Crinan Street London N1 9XW
A division of Macmillan Publishers Limited
Companies and representatives throughout the world

ISBN 978-0-230-46216-8 (with key)
ISBN 978-0-230-46470-4 (without key)
ISBN 978-0-230-46218-2 (with key + MPO Pack)
ISBN 978-0-230-46469-8 (without key + MPO Pack)

Designed by Kamae Design, Oxford

Illustrated by Kamae Design, p6, 8, 13, 14, 16, 21, 22, 23, 24, 29, 30, 32, 33, 37, 39, 45, 47, 48, 53, 55, 57, 61, 62, 64, 69,
71, 77, 78, 85. Ed McLachlan, p54.

Cover photograph by Superstock/Blend Images
Picture research by Susannah Jayes

Authors' acknowledgements
Sam McCarter and Norman Whitby would like to thank the editors.

The publishers would like to thank all those who participated in the development of the project, with special thanks
to the freelance editors.

The authors and publishers would like to thank the following for permission to reproduce their photographs:
Alamy/Blend Images p16(cr), Alamy/the box studio p79, Alamy/Judith Collins p6(4), Alamy/EIGHTFISH p81,
Alamy/Enigma p46(tl), Alamy/eye35 p30(cl), Alamy/I. Glory p66, Alamy/Andrew Holt p38(a), Alamy/D. Hurst p14(b),
Alamy/Image Source p51, Alamy/Emmanuel LATTES p38(c), Alamy/MBI p70(cm), Alamy/Jeff Morgan 05 p16(cm),
Alamy/Stockbroker p43, Alamy/Maksym Yemelyanov p10(tl), Alamy/Justin Kase zsixz p70(cl); **Bananastock** p60;
The Bridgeman Art Library/Photo © Christie's Images p14(c); **Corbis**/Auslöser p28, Corbis/Bettmann p58(a),
Corbis/Fraser Hall p38(b), Corbis/Troy House p59(cr), Corbis/David Howells p6(1), Corbis/Tim Pannell p27; **Digital
Vision** p10(tr); **Getty Images** p62(d), Getty Images/Tim Bewer p46(bl), Getty Images/Fuse p34, Getty Images/
Richard Gilliard p62(c), Getty Images/Troels Graugaard p42, Getty Images/Thomas Kokta p78(a), Getty Images/
Barrett & MacKay p62(b), Getty Images/José Fuste Raga p12, Getty Images/Stockbyte p78(b), Getty Images/
View Stock p14(e), Getty Images/Stephan Zabel p16(cl); **Macmillan Publishers Limited**/David Tolley p14(a);
The National Archives/© Crown Copyright 2012 p85; **Rex Features**/Tom Dymond p58(b), Rex Features/Nils
Jorgensen p70(cr); **Science Photo Library**/Mark de Freye p75; **David Simonds**/The Economist p54; **Superstock**/
Nano Calvo/age fotostock p50(tr), Superstock/Cusp p76; **Thinkstock**/Istockphoto pp6(2,3),10(tc),14(d),26,30(cr),5
0(cr),59(bcr),62(a).

The authors and the publishers are grateful for permission to reprint the following copyright material:
Benson, E. (2003, February). Intelligence across cultures. *Monitor on Psychology*, 34(2). Retrieved from *www.apa.
org/monitor/*. Copyright © 2003 by the American Psychological Association; used with approval;
Extracts 'Coffee rust' and 'Why Europeans Drink Tea' by Gail L Schumann both taken from *www.apsnet.org*.
Copyright © The American Phytopathological Society, reprinted by permission of the publisher;
Extract from 'Geothermal Energy Facts: Introductory Level and Advanced Level' taken from *www.geothermal.
marin.org*, reprinted by permission of Geothermal Education Office, 664 Hilary Drive, Tiburon, CA 94920, USA;
Extract from 'Youth: The Future of Travel' taken from UN World Tourism Affiliate Members Report Volume 2, ©
UNWTO, 9284402513, reprinted with approval;
Glinkowski P, Bamford A. Insight and Exchange: An evaluation of the Wellcome Trust's Sciart programme. London:
Wellcome Trust; 2009. *www.wellcome.ac.uk/sciartevaluation*, reprinted with approval.

Printed and bound in Thailand

2018 2017 2016 2015
10 9 8 7 6 5 4 3

Contents

Introduction
page 4

	Topic	Task 1	Task 2
Unit 1 page 6	**Change and consequences**	Describing trends Using nouns to summarize Understanding data	Understanding questions Expressing solutions Using linking devices Using trigger words
Unit 2 page 14	**The importance of the past**	Comparing information Using adverbs in comparisons Comparing and contrasting	Using *it/they/this/these* Planning essays Developing ideas
Unit 3 page 22	**Machines, cycles and processes**	Using the passive Sequencing	Using *which* to organize and add information Expressing result and purpose
Unit 4 page 30	**Education**	Using general and specific statements Paraphrasing Describing proportions	Avoiding overgeneralization Developing reasons
Unit 5 page 38	**Youth**	Describing changes Describing locations	Developing and justifying opinions Writing introductions
Unit 6 page 46	**Culture**	Writing overviews Describing two sets of data Using complex sentences: Concession (1)	Expressing advantages and disadvantages Using advantage and disadvantage vocabulary Using complex sentences: Concession (2)
Unit 7 page 54	**Arts and sciences**	Using adverbs Using adverbs to evaluate data Avoiding irrelevance	Discussing other people's opinions Hypothesizing
Unit 8 page 62	**Nature**	Making predictions Ensuring factual accuracy Making predictions in the past	Using articles Writing conclusions
Unit 9 page 70	**Health**	Paraphrasing and using synonyms Checking spelling	Using general nouns to link and summarize ideas Using cause and effect relationships Ensuring verb-subject agreement
Unit 10 page 78	**The individual and society**	Using the correct word order Linking information and data using *with* Task 1 revision	Using the appropriate paragraph structure Distinguishing between relevant and irrelevant information Task 2 revision

Model and sample answers
page 86

Answer Key
page 97

Introduction

What is *Improve your IELTS Writing Skills?*

Improve your IELTS Writing Skills is a complete preparation course for students at score bands 4.5–6.00 preparing for the Academic Writing paper of the International English Language Testing System. Through targeted practice, it develops skills and language to help you achieve a higher IELTS score in the Academic Writing paper.

How can I use this book?

You can use *Improve your IELTS Writing Skills* as a book for studying on your own or in a class.

If you are studying on your own, *Improve your IELTS Writing Skills* is designed to guide you step by step through the activities. This book is also completely self-contained: a clear and accessible key is provided so that you can easily check your answers as you work through the book. In addition, there is either a sample answer written by a student or a model answer written by the authors to accompany each Task 1 and Task 2 question.

If you are studying as part of a class, your teacher will direct you on how to use each activity. Some activities can be treated as discussions, in which case they can be a useful opportunity to share ideas and techniques with other learners.

How is *Improve your IELTS Writing Skills* organized?

It consists of ten units based around topics which occur commonly in the real test.

Each unit consists of three sections:

Task 1: exercises and examples to develop skills and language for Task 1 questions.

Task 2: exercises and examples to develop skills and language for Task 2 questions.

Practice test: a complete Academic Writing paper based on the unit topic to practise the skills learned.

Each Task 1 and Task 2 section is subdivided further into skills sections. These focus on specific areas of relevance to each task.

In addition, there are Technique boxes throughout the book. These reinforce key points on how to approach Academic Writing tasks.

How will *Improve your IELTS Writing Skills* improve my score?

By developing skills

The skills sections form a detailed syllabus of essential IELTS writing skills. For example, key elements of Task 1 preparation, such as *Describing trends* and *Comparing information*, are fully covered. Similarly, Task 2 skills, such as *Expressing solutions* and *Developing ideas*, are dealt with in detail.

By developing language

Each unit also contains a resource of useful phrases and vocabulary to use in each writing task. Over the course of *Improve your IELTS Writing Skills*, you will encounter a wide range of ideas to ensure that you are not lost for words when you get to the real test. These include concepts such as organizing words, trigger words and linking phrases, which all contribute to an appropriate academic writing style.

By developing test technique

The Technique boxes contain short tips which can easily be memorized and used as reminders in the real test. These include quick and easy advice about planning, understanding questions and how to use effectively the language you have learned.

How is the IELTS Academic Writing component organized?

The Academic Writing component of the IELTS lasts one hour. In the test, there are two tasks of different lengths, both of which you must answer.

What does each task consist of?

In Task 1, you will have to write at least 150 words to describe some data or a diagram. Data will normally be presented in the form of a graph, a bar or pie chart, a table or a combination of these. A diagram will normally relate to a process, the workings of an object or changes in maps over time. You are always expected to summarize the information by describing the main features, making comparisons where relevant.

In Task 2, you will have to write at least 250 words on a topic. You will be presented with an opinion, an argument or a problem and you will be expected to respond in some way. For example, in your response, you may be asked to:

- Express an opinion.
- Give views about two different opinions and give your own opinion.
- Discuss advantages and disadvantages.
- Give a solution to a problem by suggesting measures.
- Discuss causes of a problem and suggest solutions.

You are always expected to give reasons and include any relevant examples from your own knowledge and experience.

How will I be assessed?

In both tasks you will be assessed on your ability to express yourself clearly and accurately in English.

In Task 1, your answer is assessed according to your ability to write about data in an organized way and compare information where it is relevant to do so. You should write about the main features of the data and add relevant detail where necessary.

In Task 2, your answer is assessed according to your ability to write in a logical manner as you give a solution to a problem, present and justify an opinion, compare and contrast evidence and opinions or evaluate and challenge ideas or arguments.

How much time should I spend on each task?

You are advised to spend 20 minutes on Task 1.

You are advised to spend 40 minutes on Task 2.

Even though Task 2 carries more marks, you should always do Task 1 first. This is because it is shorter, and psychologically it feels better if you have completed one task.

1

Change
and consequences

UNIT AIMS

| TASK 1 | Describing trends
Using nouns to summarize
Understanding data | TASK 2 | Understanding questions
Expressing solutions
Using linking devices
Using trigger words |

1

2

3

4

TASK 1 Describing trends

a

1 Name items 1–4 above.

b
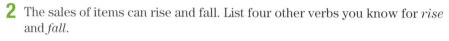

2 The sales of items can rise and fall. List four other verbs you know for *rise* and *fall*.

Rise _____

Fall _____

c

3 The graphs a–h relate to sales of media technology.
Which graph do you think shows sales for each item in the photos 1–4?

d

4 Match each graph (a–h) with the most appropriate description (1–10) below.
Some graphs will be used more than once.

   1 Sales of audio cassettes fell steadily. *g*
   2 iPod sales rose gradually. _____
   3 Plasma TV sales fluctuated wildly, but the trend was upward. _____
   4 Sales of video cassettes fluctuated wildly and the trend was downward.
     _____

e
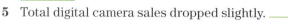

   5 Total digital camera sales dropped slightly. _____
   6 Sales of audio cassettes fell and then levelled off. _____
   7 The sales of tablets rose gradually and then climbed sharply. _____
   8 Purchases of video cassette recorders declined dramatically. _____
f
   9 Sales of games consoles decreased and then levelled off. _____
   10 CD sales dropped suddenly. _____

5 Underline all the verbs in exercise 4 used to describe trends.
Example
1 Sales of audio cassettes <u>fell</u> steadily.

g

6 In the sentences in exercise 4, adverbs such as *steadily* describe the verbs.
Find the adverbs and decide whether they mean slow or fast changes.
Complete the lists below.

Slow _____
h
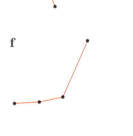

Fast _____

Using nouns to summarize

1 Provide the noun form of the verbs below.

> fall ■ rise ■ increase ■ decline ■ drop ■ fluctuate ■ improve ■ reduce ■ grow

> ### Technique
>
> Use nouns instead of verbs to summarize information and add variety to your writing. You can often rewrite sentences containing verb phrases such as *fell steadily* by using the correct form of *there is/are* and the correct use of the appropriate noun.
>
> *Examples*
> The consumption of chocolate *fell steadily*. (verb + adverb)
> There was *a steady fall* in the consumption of chocolate. *(there was a + adjective + noun)*
> There has been *a dramatic rise* in the production of films. *(there has been a + adjective + noun)*
> The production of films *has risen dramatically*. (verb + adverb)

2 Read the examples in the Technique box. Then rewrite sentences a–j below.

   a Spice exports from Africa fluctuated wildly over the period.

     There were _____

   b The development of new products fell gradually.

     There was _____

   c There has been a noticeable decrease in research investment.

     Research investment _____

   d The purchases of tickets dropped significantly last month.

     There was _____

   e On the Internet, the number of sites rose dramatically.

     There was _____

   f There was a sudden decrease in the sale of mangos.

     The sale _____

   g At the theme park, there were very slight fluctuations in the number of visitors.

     The number _____

   h There was a gradual decline in sugar imports.

     Sugar imports _____

   i The quality of food in supermarkets has increased slowly.

     There has _____

   j The number of air travellers fluctuated remarkably.

     There _____

3 Phrases such as *the consumption of chocolate* can often be rewritten as just two or three nouns. Read the examples below. Then find and rewrite eight other examples in exercise 2.

Examples
The consumption of chocolate can become *Chocolate consumption*.
The production of films can become *Film production*. (not *Films production*)

> ### Technique
>
> Include a variety of structures in your writing: noun + noun (*sugar imports*) and the noun + *of* + noun (*the import of sugar*).

Understanding data

1 Look at the graph below and the Task 1 question.

What was the income in dollars for:

a The Tea Room in January? _____

b Internet Express in July? _____

c Wi-fi Café in November? _____

d Café Cool in December? _____

e The Tea Room in February? _____

In which month did:

f Café Cool earn the most money? _____

g Wi-fi Café earn the least money? _____

Task 1

You should spend about 20 minutes on this task.

The graph shows the income of four cafés in New York over last year.

Summarize the information by selecting and reporting the main features. Make comparisons where relevant.

Write at least 150 words.

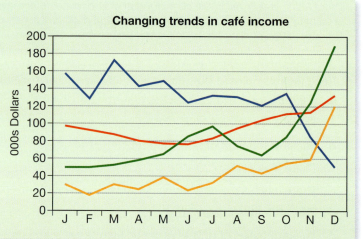

Changing trends in café income

2 Answer these questions about the graph.

a What do the letters J, F, M, etc, along the bottom of the graph mean?

b What does 000s mean?

c What patterns can you see?

d What comparisons can you make?

> **Technique**
>
> Write the names of the cafés at the end of each line to help you read the graph.

3 Read the text below and decide whether each of the seven missing phrases is a verb, a noun or an adverb.

Example

1 adverb

The graph provides information about the income trends of four cafés over the last year.

Overall, although the income for all four cafés showed some fluctuation from month to month, we can identify some general upward and downward trends. As regards the earnings for The Tea Room, they were down over the year, falling **1** _____ from almost $160,000 earnings a month to around $50,000 in December.

By contrast, the income for the other three cafés went up by varying degrees. There was **2** _____ in Café Cool's sales over the first ten months, followed by a sudden increase to $120,000. Furthermore, the income for both Internet Express and the Wi-fi Café **3** _____ in December. The former experienced **4** _____ to June but, after that, income rose **5** _____ , ending the year at approximately $130,000. Likewise, the trend for Wi-fi Café was upward. Between January and July, earnings **6** _____ from $50,000 to nearly $100,000 and **7** _____ to around $190,000.

It is noticeable that the income for The Tea Room is lower in the winter months than for the other three cafés.

4 Match options a–g with gaps 1–7 in the text. Use the graph to help you.

a steadily
b then rocketed
c doubled
d significantly

e also went up
f a steady fall
g a rise

5 Find the following in the text in exercise 3.

a A phrase to introduce a new item on the graph.
b A phrase to show you are going to talk about a different trend from the one in the previous sentence.
c Two phrases to show you are going to talk about a similar trend to the one in the previous sentence.

TASK 2 Understanding questions

1 In each group a–d below, which general noun has a different meaning from the other two?

a advantages drawbacks benefits

b measures steps reasons

c causes effects consequences

d disadvantages drawbacks solutions

> ### Technique
> Learn to analyse Task 2 questions. They contain a general subject and often include a general noun or nouns to help you organize your essay, e.g. *The world is changing rapidly* (general subject). *What are the causes* (general noun to help you organize your answer) *of this*?

2 Complete each Task 2 question below with the general nouns and verbs from the box. You may use each item more than once.

> agree or disagree ▪ advantages ▪ disadvantages ▪ causes
> solutions ▪ measures ▪ views ▪ ~~benefits~~

a What are the _____*benefits*_____ of learning skills in the modern world?

b Any attempts to preserve the natural world will always hinder economic development. However the benefits of helping the environment will always far outweigh the _____ . Do you _____ ?

c Some young people take a year off between school and university. What are the _____ and _____ of taking such time off?

d Students should be trained on how to cope with changes in the modern world. How far do you _____ ?

e Volunteer work with disadvantaged groups like underprivileged children is the best way for young people to learn about the real world. To what extent do you _____ ? What other _____ could be effective?

f Every day, animals are becoming extinct throughout the world. What do you think the _____ of this are? What _____ can you suggest to deal with this?

g Some people think overcrowding in large cities can be reduced by building skyscrapers, while others think the problem can be solved by encouraging people to move to the countryside. Discuss both these _____ and give your own opinion.

> ### Technique
> Number the parts of the task and tick them as you do them.

3 How many parts are there in each question in exercise 2? For example, (a) has one part. If there are two or three parts, how are they related?

Unit 1

Expressing solutions

1 Change is more rapid in the modern world than it was in the past. Use the three pictures below to help you think of some changes which have taken place in the last 30 years.

2 Number each area below 1–5 according to how rapidly you think each one is changing (1 = most rapid; 5 = least rapid). Think of an example of rapid change for each category.

> Work ■ Technology ■ Travel ■ Communication ■ Health

3 Write a sentence for each area in exercise 2.

Example

Work is the area where change is the most rapid.

4 Look at the Task 2 question below and answer questions a–c.

> ### Task 2
>
> *You should spend about 40 minutes on this task.*
>
> *Write about the following topic.*
>
> **More and more people claim that modern work patterns are a source of stress. What do you think are the causes of this? Can you suggest some possible solutions?**
>
> *Give reasons for your answer and include any relevant examples from your own knowledge or experience.*

   a Which part of the question states a problem?
   b Which two words in the question are important for the organization of your answer?
   c What else do the instructions tell you to include in your answer?

5 Read the conversation between two students discussing the problem of stress at work. Which part of the question in exercise 4 are they answering? What solutions and results do they suggest?

Shen:	How do you think people can deal with their stressful lives, especially at work?
Tina:	Firstly, I think employers should encourage workers to relax.
Shen:	How?
Tina:	Well, in some companies, gym facilities or massage therapies are available.
Shen:	A massage?
Tina:	Yes. It can help employees to relax. This improves their efficiency and productivity.
Shen:	Are there other solutions?
Tina:	Of course. Employees could be trained in how to plan their time more effectively. One way is to stop people taking work home. And then the workplace will become a lot happier.

6 The paragraph below suggests a solution to the Task 2 question. Complete each gap with one of phrases a–f below.

a A further step is to
b for example
c I think the most obvious solution is

d As a result
e By doing this
f For instance

> **1** _____ for employers to encourage workers to relax.
> **2** _____ , in some companies, gym facilities or massage therapies are available. **3** _____ , this improves their efficiency and production. **4** _____ train employees in how to plan their time more effectively, **5** _____ , by stopping people taking work home. **6** _____ , the workplace will become a lot happier.

Technique

Identify the type of question in the Task. For cause/solution question types, include both and give reasons and examples. Organize each idea into an appropriate paragraph structure using linking words.

7 Read the examples from exercises 5 and 6. Then rewrite the sentences in a–f.

Examples

Employers should encourage *workers to relax.*

I think the most obvious solution is for employers to encourage *workers to relax.*

Employees could be trained *how to plan their time more effectively.*

A further step is to train employees *how to plan their time more effectively.*

Technique

Use different ways to express solutions to add variety to your answer.

Use *should* for strong suggestions; *could* and *might* are used for possible suggestions. Other phrases you can use are: *Another/further + solution/step/possibility/measure/approach/way is to …* Conditional sentences are also useful to talk about problems and solutions.

a I think the most obvious solution is to encourage people to exercise more.

People should _____

b The answer is to reduce the number of working hours.

The number of working hours _____

c The government could provide each employee with their own computer.

One possibility is _____

d One option is to persuade parents to spend more time with their children.

Parents could _____

e A good idea is to restrict the number of cars coming into cities.

The number of cars coming into cities _____

f The government should build more skyscrapers to solve the problem.

If the government _____

8 Which problems of modern life in the box do the sentences in exercise 7 refer to?

> overcrowding ■ traffic congestion ■ obesity ■ lack of discipline ■ stress ■ lack of technology

9 Use the following phrases to add results to the solutions above. Use your own ideas and words.

Example

a I think the most obvious solution is to encourage people to exercise more.
By doing this, they would lose weight and would feel better generally.

> As a result, ■ This would enable/help them to ■ This would lead to
> This means that they would ■ By doing this, ■ Consequently,

Unit 1

Using linking devices

1 Linking devices mark the functions of other sentences and phrases, such as solutions, results and examples. Match each linking device with the correct function.

| addition | _____ | example | _____ | reason | _____ |
| condition | _____ | purpose | _____ | result | _____ |

and ■ consequently, ■ and so ■ since ■ for instance, ■ because ■ in order to therefore, ■ if ■ furthermore, ■ as a result, ■ for example,

Using trigger words

1 Read the paragraph from a Task 2 essay on overcrowded cities and find the linking devices which match these functions.

Reason ■ Result ■ Example ■ Solution

Many cities in the world have now become very overcrowded because people are migrating in from the countryside in search of work. As a result, facilities like water supplies and public transport cannot cope with the demands from increased numbers of people and so they are under severe strain. The obvious answer is to encourage the creation of jobs outside the cities. For example, we could encourage certain businesses to set up branches in rural areas.

2 Linking devices can be used to trigger ideas because they mark functions. Use the trigger words below to develop the ideas given.

A

If people migrate to cities, they become _____ .

And so _____ .

And as a result _____ .

A good idea would be to _____ .

By doing this, _____ .

B

People spend too much time watching TV.

For example, _____ .

Consequently, _____ .

If _____ , then _____ .

This could lead to _____ .

C

The development of tourism often creates negative feeling among local people because _____ .

For example, _____ .

The obvious answer is to _____ .

Furthermore, _____ .

Technique

Use linking devices to trigger your own ideas and to organize them. Also use them to guide the reader through your writing. When you are planning a Task 2 answer, write down some trigger words to help you develop your basic idea.

Practice Test 1

Task 1

You should spend about 20 minutes on this task.

The graph below shows the changing patterns of access to modern technology in homes in the UK (expressed in percentage terms).

Summarize the information by selecting and reporting the main features and make comparisons where relevant.

Write at least 150 words.

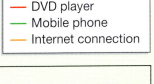

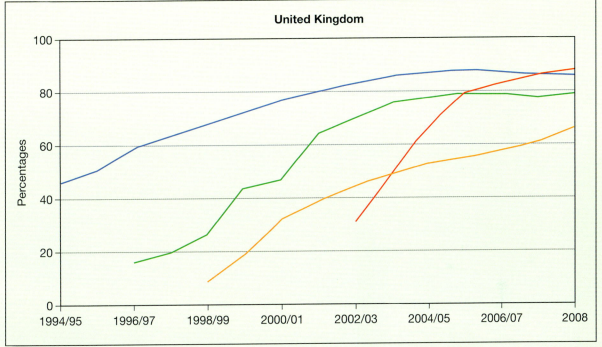

Task 1 Checklist

1 Paraphrase the rubric in the introduction, i.e, change the words and the structure where possible.

2 Write an overview after your introduction or at the end.

3 Include all the data at the beginning and ends of lines.

4 Use linking devices.

5 Use nouns and verbs to describe the trends.

6 Write at least 150 words.

7 Use at least three paragraphs.

8 Check your answer for mistakes.

Task 2

You should spend about 40 minutes on this task.

Write about the following topic:

People often find it difficult to adapt to new situations in their lives.

Why do you think this is? What measures can you suggest to make it easier?

Give reasons for your answer and include any relevant examples from your own knowledge or experience.

Write at least 250 words.

UNIT AIMS

TASK 1 Comparing information
Using adverbs in comparisons
Comparing and contrasting

TASK 2 Using *it/they/this/these*
Planning essays
Developing ideas

a
Ballpoint pen,
Laszlo Biro

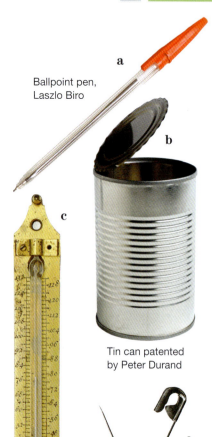

b

Tin can patented
by Peter Durand

d

Safety pin, Walter Hunt

c

First mercury
thermometer,
Gabriel
Fahrenheit

e

Paper money in China

TASK 1 Comparing information

1 The pictures and text show some inventions and who invented them. Answer the questions.

a   Which is the oldest invention?
b   Which is the most recent invention?
c   Which do you think are the most and least important inventions?
d   What other important historical inventions are not included here?
e   What do you think are the three most effective inventions in recent years?

2 The chart shows the results of a survey about the most important inventions in the last 300 years. Answer the questions.

Most important inventions in the last 300 years

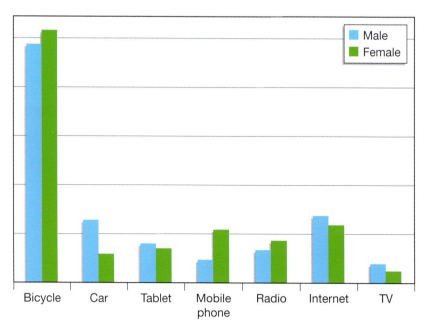

a   What is the most noticeable thing about the chart?
b   What voting patterns can you see for females?
c   What voting patterns can you see for males?
d   Do you agree with the survey results? Why/Why not?

Technique

Circle and number important data on the chart that you are going to write about. Group data that you want to write about together or compare (e.g. by labelling them 2a, 2b, 2c).

3 Complete sentences a–j about the chart in exercise 2 on page 14, using the structures in the Technique box.

a   More females _____ males chose the bicycle.

b   The bicycle was more _____ than any other invention.

c   The car was _____ popular among females than males.

d   _____ invention among both sexes was the TV.

e   _____ women than men voted for the mobile phone.

f   _____ invention among both sexes was the bicycle.

g   _____ males than females picked the radio.

h   The tablet was _____ for women than for men.

i   More people selected the bicycle _____ any other invention.

j   The TV was _____ popular than any other invention.

Technique

Use a range of structures to make comparisons. Read these examples that describe the chart in exercise 2.

Examples
- *More* males *than* females chose the TV. (*more* + noun + *than*)
- *Fewer* females *than* males chose the TV. (*fewer* + noun + *than*)
- The TV *was more popular* among males *than* females. (*more/less* + adjective + *than*)
- The *most popular* form of communication was the Internet. (*the most/least* + adjective)

4 Rewrite the sentences in exercise 3 using the following words: (a) fewer males (b) the most (c) more popular (d) less popular (e) fewer (f) more … than (g) more (h) more (i) the most (j) the least

Example

a   *Fewer males than females chose the bicycle.*

5 Compare male and female attitudes to bicycles, cars, tablets, mobile phones and the Internet.

Examples
Almost *as many* females *as* males chose the tablet.
Not as many males *as* females chose the radio.

Technique

Compare information by using *as many … as* when numbers are very close, or by using *not as many … as*. Read the examples in exercise 5.

6 Make comparative sentences based on notes a–g below and the chart in exercise 2. Use the passive or active form of the verb in italics.

Examples
females/males/*select*/the bicycle *More females than males selected the bicycle.*
males/females/*select*/the bicycle *Fewer males than females selected the bicycle.*
the bicycle/*choose*/females/males *The bicycle was chosen by more females than males.*

a   males/females/*choose*/the car

_____

b   women/men/*select*/the mobile phone

_____

c   the Internet/*choose*/males/females

_____

d   females/males/*pick*/the radio

_____

e   males/females/*pick*/the radio

_____

f   the tablet/*choose*/females/males

_____

g   the bicycle/*select*/males/females

_____

Unit 2

Using adverbs in comparisons

1 Read the examples. Then underline the adverbs in sentences a–i.

   a Slightly more women than men voted for the bicycle.

   b In the past, considerably more people lived in the countryside than towns.

   c Many more people can use a computer today than thirty years ago.

   d Substantially less time is now spent doing housework than before.

   e There are significantly fewer people now working in manufacturing than in the past.

   f Sports programmes are watched by practically as many people now as in previous years.

   g The exhibition about cinema attracted far fewer visitors than expected.

   h Illiteracy is much less common than in previous generations.

   i Nearly as many children as adults watch programmes about ancient history.

2 Which adverbs in exercise 1 mean:

   a almost?   **b** a lot?   **c** just a few?

3 Add suitable adverbs to the sentences you wrote in exercise 6 on page 15.

> ### Technique
> Add adverbs to comparisons, such as *significantly (more)* or *almost (as many)* to make them more precise.
>
> #### Examples
> - *Significantly more* people voted for the bicycle than the other inventions.
> - The bicycle was chosen by *almost as many* males *as* females.

Comparing and contrasting

1 What kinds of clubs do people join? Do you belong to any clubs?

2 What kinds of clubs are shown in the photos below?

3 Find the clubs that you named in exercise 1 on the chart opposite. Answer the following about the bar chart.

   a What does the bar chart provide information about?

   b What could the numbers on the left relate to?

   c What do you think the words along the bottom of the chart relate to?

   d What do the numbers in the box in the top left of the chart refer to?

   e Is there a time reference for the graph?

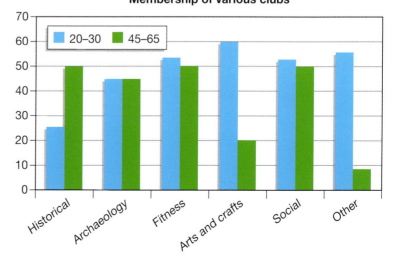
Membership of various clubs

4 Make at least three questions about the data. Then ask your questions to a partner.

Example
Which club or society has the most people aged 20–30?

5 Match sentence beginnings 1–6 with endings a–f to form correct sentences about the chart.

  1 The arts and crafts club has the greatest number of 20–30 year-olds,
  2 Only 25 people from the younger age group are members of the historical club,
  3 Some clubs are clearly more popular with one of the age groups,
  4 The fitness and social clubs have slightly more members in the younger age group,
  5 In general, the 20–30 year-olds are more actively involved in clubs
  6 The fitness and social clubs attract a broader range of people

  a *whereas* the archaeological club is equally popular with both.
  b *in comparison with* the historical club.
  c *but* it is one of the least popular clubs with the older age group.
  d *compared with* the older age bracket.
  e *while* the figure for 45–65 year-olds is about 50.
  f *although* they are fairly popular with both age groups.

6 In which of the sentences in exercise 5 could the ending a–f come first? Which connecting words in italics are followed by a noun phrase only?

7 Read the following description of the chart you looked at in exercise 3. In 1–6, two options are possible and one is incorrect. Delete the incorrect option.

The chart provides information about how two age groups participate in several clubs at a centre for adults. We can see from the data that the archaeological, fitness and social clubs are popular with both older and younger people. **1** *While/However/By contrast*, the historical and arts and crafts societies clearly appeal more to one of the age groups. In the historical society, 50 of the members are between 45 and 65, **2** *but/while/however* there are only 25 from the younger age group. For the arts and crafts society, the pattern is reversed.
There are about 60 members aged between 20 and 30, **3** *but/whereas in comparison with* the number of people in the 45 to 65 age group is **4** *far/slightly/considerably* lower.
The fitness and social clubs are popular with both age groups, **5** *however/but/although* there are slightly fewer older people. Membership of the archaeological society stands at 45 for both groups.
In general, the younger age group are **6** *significantly/almost/noticeably* more involved in the various societies than the 45–65 year-olds.

TASK 2 Using it/they/this/these

1 Read the text opposite written by a student as part of a Task 2 answer. Replace the words in italics with *it*, *they*, *this* or *these*.

> Archaeologists, for example, help us to learn about the past. *Archaeologists* look for evidence in artefacts like pots and jewellery. *Pots and jewellery* reveal a lot of information about our ancestors. *Revealing information about the past* is very useful, but *the information* is still quite limited.

2 Match 1–4 with a–d to explain how to use *it*, *they*, *this* and *these*.

1 *It* and *this* refer to	**a** nouns and phrases at the end of the previous sentence.
2 *They* and *these* refer to	**b** plural nouns.
3 *This* and *these* are often used to refer to	**c** situations and processes.
4 *This* can also refer to	**d** singular nouns.

3 Underline the exact text which *it*, *they*, *this* and *these* refer to in sentences a–h. The first one has been done for you.

a History teaches <u>children</u> not just facts, but a range of skills. For example, *they* can learn how to analyse material, do basic sorting and research.

b Old buildings help create a more relaxing environment in cities than concrete office blocks. *This* makes them more pleasant to work and live in.

c Studying history may trigger an interest in other subject areas. *This*, in turn, may lead to different hobbies.

d Built-up areas can be made more attractive by adding monuments and statues. *These* can then enrich people's lives considerably.

e Governments should provide more money to preserve historical sites. By doing *this*, our heritage would be saved for future generations.

f Tradition does not hold us back as some people believe. In fact, *it* helps us to build the future.

g Schools and colleges need to emphasize history and related subjects as *these* will help give them a wider view of the world.

h The Internet and computers can be used to preserve the past. For example, *they* can be used by children to do basic research and store images.

4 Complete sentences a–g with *it*, *they*, *this* or *these*. Some answers have more than one option.

a If the past is to be preserved, _____ must be done by using modern technology.

b The art and language of a country represent its history, so it is important that _____ are both preserved.

c The primary role of advertising is to encourage the public to replace the old with the new. _____ is called progress by some people.

d History broadens the minds of most people who study _____ , but _____ also has the potential to narrow the minds of some.

e History should be given more emphasis in school, as _____ will help children to understand better the world they live in.

f If history is emphasized more in schools, _____ will lead to a better understanding of the world.

g The past informs us of the present and the future, but few people are sufficiently aware of _____ .

5 Complete each blank space in the paragraph below with a sentence of your own. Begin each sentence using either *it*, *they*, *this* or *these* to refer back to the phrases in bold.

One of the most important developments in technology over the past decades has been **the Internet**. 1 _____ Reading a webpage is, however, not like reading a book. We **read webpages much more quickly** and **then make an immediate connection** to something on another page. 2 _____ Books are also gradually being replaced by **e-readers**. 3 _____

Planning essays

1 Read the historical facts in a–f below. Rank the events 1–6 according to how important you think they were in human history (1 = most important; 6 = least important). What other events would you add to the list?

   a In 1792, France abolished the monarchy and replaced it with the first republic.
   b In 1953, Francis Watson and James Crick described the structure and importance of DNA.
   c In October 1492, Christopher Columbus set foot in the Americas.
   d In 1885, Karl Benz built and patented the first automobile.
   e In 1983, a computer system connecting universities was created, which later became the Internet.
   f In the ninth century, gunpowder was first invented and used by the Chinese.

2 Read the Task 2 essay question below.

> *It is sometimes said that history never repeats itself, yet there is much in it which is relevant to our modern world. In what ways can the study of history help us today?*

Decide which of points a–g are relevant to the answer to this question.

   a There is often uncertainty about what really happened with regard to well-known historical events.
   b Studying other historical periods gives insights into different ways of life.
   c We can learn about the recent past by asking older family members.
   d History involves investigation and interpretation, so its study develops thinking skills.
   e Learning about conflicts in the past can teach us how to avoid them in future.
   f History is a more difficult area of study than most people imagine.
   g The past can often provide explanations for the situations we face today.

3 Read the statement below and use the trigger words in a–d to develop this point. The first one has been done for you. Refer to Unit 1 page 12 for more examples of similar phrases.

Studying other historical periods gives insights into different ways of life.

For example, *students can investigate the way in which people lived in ancient times.*

such as _____

As a result, _____

Therefore, _____

Furthermore, _____

4 Look back at the other relevant sentences you chose in exercise 2 above. Develop those ideas in the same way using trigger words. Then write out your ideas in a paragraph.

Developing ideas

1 Read the Task 2 question below. Make a note of any ways you can think of to make history more interesting.

> *Some children find learning history at school very exciting but many others think it is very boring. In what ways can history be brought to life for all schoolchildren?*

2 The list a–i below contains ideas that a student came up with for the essay question in exercise 1. There are three solutions, each with an example and an effect. Complete the table by matching each idea with the appropriate function.

	Paragraph 1	Paragraph 2	Paragraph 3
Solutions	*a*		
Examples			
Effects			

a using the Internet and computers

f it increases motivation to do research

b visiting historical sites

g these skills can be applied in other subjects

c historical places seem more real

h doing written projects

d make a poster about local history

i search for information about historical figures online

e go to a local archaeological site

3 Decide which function in exercise 2 these linking devices relate to.

- **a** Another method is to
- **b** This will lead to
- **c** For example,
- **d** Last but not least, children could
- **e** For instance,
- **f** such as
- **g** As a result,
- **h** The best way is to
- **i** Then

Technique

Recycle relevant information from other essays to help you build a bank of ideas.

4 Use your answers to exercises 2 and 3 to write the ideas out as three paragraphs.

Practice Test 2

Task 1

You should spend about 20 minutes on this task.

The graph below shows the contribution of three sectors – agriculture, manufacturing and business and financial services – to the UK economy in the twentieth century.

Summarize the information by selecting and reporting the main features and make comparisons where relevant.

Write at least 150 words.

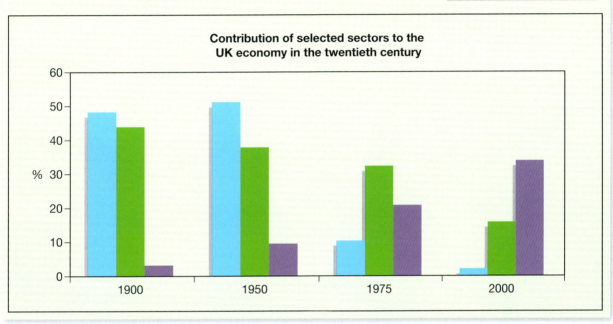

Task 2

You should spend about 40 minutes on this task.

Write about the following topic:

To some people studying the past is the best way to help young people function well in the modern world. To what extent do you agree or disagree? What other measures could be effective in helping young people to function well in the modern world?

Give reasons for your answer and include any relevant examples from your own knowledge or experience.

Write at least 250 words.

Task 2 Checklist

1 Before you start writing, decide how many paragraphs (usually about 5, including an introduction and conclusion) you are going to have.

2 Use trigger words like *because*, *the reason is* to get some ideas for possible causes.

3 Look at your causes and think of one or two measures to go with each particular cause.

4 Keep the introduction short – no more than two or three sentences.

5 Write a conclusion, summarizing your essay.

Task 1 Using the passive

1 Look at the five objects a–e and answer the questions.

   a Which of these materials are used to make these objects?

> wood ▪ plastic ▪ cement ▪ bricks ▪ diamonds
> metal ▪ leather ▪ glass ▪ rubber

   b Which of the materials in your list are natural and which are manufactured?

2 Complete 1–6 with the correct forms of the verbs in brackets.

Examples

A river *runs* through London. (active)

Many electronic goods are *manufactured* in Japan. (passive: *be* + past participle)

> ### Manufacturing cement
> Limestone is the main ingredient of cement. Firstly, it **1** _____ (extract) from the ground. Then, at the factory, it **2** _____ (heat) to a high temperature with other ingredients. After this, it **3** _____ (cool) with blasts of cold air.

> ### How rain is formed
> When warm air **4** (reach) high ground, it is forced to rise, and, as a result, it **5** (cool). Moisture in the air **6** (condense) to form rain.

3 Complete 1–8 with the correct forms of the verbs in brackets.

The water table

Some rocks **1** _____ (hold) large amounts of water. When it **2** _____ (rain), the tiny spaces in the rock gradually **3** _____ (fill) with water so that the rock **4** _____ (become) saturated or full up. The top of this saturated zone is called the water table. If long periods of rain **5** _____ (occur), the water table **6** _____ (rise). If there is no rain, the rock **7** _____ (begin) to dry out and the water table **8** _____ (fall).

a

b

c

d

e

Technique
Make sure you use the correct form of the verb when you describe processes. Natural processes are often described using the active form, whereas manufacturing processes are usually described using the passive.

Natural processes:

A river *flows* from its source to the ocean. (active)

The Sun heats the water. The water evaporates.

Manufacturing processes:

Many electronic goods *are manufactured* in Japan. (passive: *be* + past participle)

The tree is chopped down. A door is made from wood.

Technique
Make sure the subject and verb agree when you describe processes.

The Sun *shines* and the temperature *rises*.

4 Are the verbs in sentences a–c transitive, intransitive, or both? Which sentence cannot be put into the passive?

a The temperature *falls*.
b Manufacturers *make* rubber products.
c Sunlight *opens* the leaves. The leaves *open*.

5 Label each verb in the box transitive (T), intransitive (I) or both (B). The first one has been done for you.

| fall *I* | ■ design | ■ produce | ■ rise | ■ send | ■ begin | ■ manufacture |
| obtain | ■ die | ■ become | ■ dry | ■ grow | ■ cool |

6 Use the notes below to write short paragraphs about production processes.

Example
The production of a car involves various stages. car/design; prototype/make; car/mass-produce; car/distribute; car/sell

The production of a car involves various stages. After the car is designed, a prototype is made and the car is mass-produced. The car is then distributed and sold.

a The production of a motorcycle involves various stages. motorcycle/design; prototype/make; prototype/test; motorcycle/manufacture; motorcycle/ export; motorcycle/sell.
b The diagram shows the various stages in the production of bread. wheat/plant; crop/harvest; wheat/transport to the mill; wheat/make flour; flour/ buy/baker; bread/bake; bread/sold.

7 Some diagrams require descriptions using past tenses. Complete the paragraph with the verbs from the box.

| **a** died and dropped **b** was formed **c** lived **d** was covered **e** was trapped **f** turned **g** is now mined **h** built up |

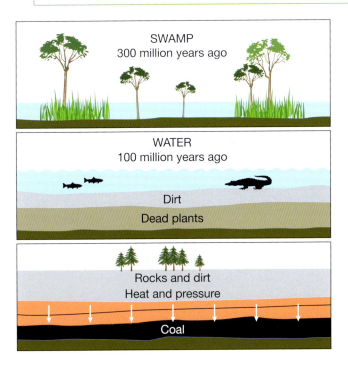

SWAMP
300 million years ago

WATER
100 million years ago

Dirt
Dead plants

Rocks and dirt
Heat and pressure

Coal

The diagrams show the process by which coal **1** _____ over a period of millions of years. First of all, large plants **2** _____ in enormous swamps a long time ago. These **3** _____ to the bottom of the water. Over the years, the dead plants formed a layer, which became deeper and deeper. More and more earth and dirt **4** _____ on top of this layer. Subsequently, this layer **5** _____ by rocks and dirt and so the energy of the dead plants **6** _____ underneath. As the pressure and the heat grew over time, the layer of dead plants **7** _____ into coal. Seams of coal were formed and coal **8** _____ .

8 Underline the active verbs in the text and double underline the passive verbs in the text in exercise 7.

Unit 3

Sequencing

1 The diagram below shows how energy is produced from coal. Answer the questions.

   a Where does the coal come from?
   b How is the coal carried to the power plant?
   c What is added to the furnace in addition to coal?
   d What gas is produced when coal is burnt in the furnace?
   e What do you think is removed from the gas?
   f What is the gas called following this process?
   g What do you think the gas does in the turbine?
   h What does the turbine do to the generator?
   i Where do the hot exhaust gases come from?
   j What happens to the gases?

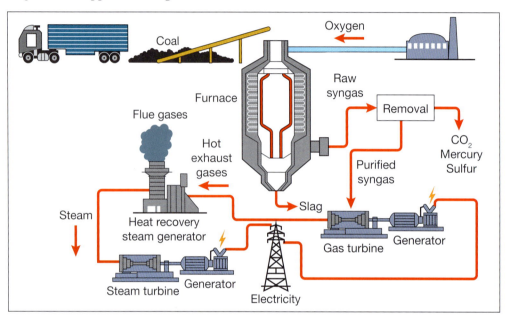

2 Write headings for each stage of the process using these verbs: deliver, add, remove, produce, convert, generate.

Example
Delivering the coal/the delivery of the coal

3 Complete the model text below by choosing the correct alternative in each case.

The diagram shows the process involved in the production of energy from coal.

1 *First of all/At first/Once* the coal is delivered by lorry. **2** *Furthermore/After that/As a result*, it is carried along a conveyor belt to the power plant, **3** *when/then/where* it is burned in a large furnace to which oxygen is added. **4** *Otherwise/From this/Therefore*, raw syngas is produced. At the next stage of the process, harmful substances like carbon dioxide, mercury and sulfur are removed. **5** *Following that/Following/Subsequent*, the purified gas is used to drive a gas turbine. The turbine **6** *in turn/afterwards/therefore* powers a generator, producing electricity. The gas turbine also produces hot exhaust gases. These are **7** *then/therefore/consequently* piped to a heat recovery steam generator, which converts the heat into steam. The steam is **8** *consequently/subsequent/subsequently* used to power a steam turbine, which again is used to generate electricity.

It is clear that the production of energy from coal requires a series of stages, including the use of exhaust gases.

> **Technique**
> Use linking devices such as *First of all*, *After that* (adverbs) and *When* (conjunction) as trigger words to help you sequence ideas when you describe processes.

4 Make a list of some of the linking devices which are used in exercise 3. Use a dictionary to help you decide whether they are adverbs or conjunctions.

Adverbs _____

Conjunctions _____

5 Connect the sentences below. Use the linking devices in brackets in each case.
Example
The parts of the car are assembled. The cars are exported. (after)
After the parts of the car are assembled, the cars are exported.

a The snow falls. It covers the ground with a protective layer. (when)

_____

b Her cubs are born. The lioness licks them all over. (as soon as)

_____

c The paper is collected. It is sent for recycling. (once)

_____

d Volcanoes erupt. They send huge amounts of smoke into the air. (before)

_____

e The plants transpire. The air becomes humid. (when)

_____

f The trees are cut down. The forest is gradually destroyed. (and)

_____

6 Connect these sentences using your own words.

a The food is processed. It is packaged. It is distributed.

_____

b The cycle is completed. It repeats itself all over again.

_____

c The rubbish is collected. It is sent to a centre for sorting. It is recycled.

_____

d A new model of the bicycle is developed. The bicycle is tested.

_____

e The TV is assembled. It is sent to the shops.

_____

f The water is purified. It is bottled.

_____

g The data about the weather is collected. The information is then broadcast.

_____

h The prototype is tested. It is modified.

_____

7 From your own knowledge, write a short paragraph to describe at least one of the processes below.

  a The process of digital photography from the action of taking a photograph to displaying the image.
  b The progress of a letter or parcel from packaging to delivery.
  c The life cycle of an animal such as a butterfly or a frog.
  d The water cycle which creates clouds and rainfall.

Task 2 Using *which* to organize and add information

1 Answer the questions about the list of technologies.

computers ■ automatic doors ■ mobile phone apps ■ video games
TV remote controls ■ tablets ■ satellite navigation systems (GPS) ■ digital cameras

  a Which of the technologies can help people and which can make life more difficult?
  b Which technologies might make people more lazy?
  c Which technologies do you find annoying and which impressive?

2 Read the Task 2 question. Which two key elements must you include in your answer? Underline the general nouns which tell you this.

> A recent survey has shown that people of all ages are losing the ability to perform basic practical tasks and processes at work. What do you think are the main causes of this? What solutions can you suggest?

3 Read the following paragraph written by a student and answer questions a–e.

> People are generally losing the traditional practical skills which they need to function in everyday life. This has come about, in my opinion, because people are now so over-reliant on machines. For example, computers in one form or another perform many of the tasks that people used to do themselves, such as office functions, opening and locking doors or switching machines on and off. Consequently, workers cannot do basic practical tasks, which in turn has an impact on how to process basic information mentally when they are at work.

  a What kind of skills are people losing?
  b What is the cause of this?
  c Which examples are given?
  d What is the practical consequence of all this?
  e What is the mental consequence?
  f What type of clause does the *which* in the last sentence introduce? Use the technique box to help you. How is it different from the clause in the first sentence?

4 In each sentence below, what does the word in italics refer to?

  a People often allow the TV to do their thinking for them at home, *which* in turn has an impact on their mental performance at work.

  b People are generally losing the traditional practical skills *which* they need to function in everyday life.

Technique

Do not use a comma with *which* when it introduces essential information that identifies what you are referring to (a defining clause). Use a comma when it introduces extra non-essential information (a non-defining clause) or when it refers back to the whole idea in the previous clause.

5 Combine the following pairs of sentences using *which*. Use the correct punctuation.

  a Sometimes, computers make mistakes. This wastes valuable time and can cost money.

  _____

  b TV programmes provide people with information about the world. This information is often very useful.

  _____

  c Machines now give us more freedom. This means that we have more time for leisure activities.

  _____

  d Technology saves us more and more time. This time can be used to create more machines.

  _____

  e More and more household tasks are now carried out by robots. They will be even more common in the future.

  _____

  f Everything seems to be available at the touch of a button. This makes people expect instant responses from other people.

  _____

6 What does *which* refer to in each of your answers in exercise 5?
In which cases does the *which* clause express an effect as in exercise 4a?

> **Technique**
> Use *which* as a trigger word to add detail to your writing.

7 Combine the sentences in a–e, deciding which information is non-essential.

  Examples
  News broadcasts about world disasters, *which* are now available 24 hours a day, can make people feel anxious.
  The situation, *which* people blame the government for, is everyone's fault.

  a The situation has now become much more complex. It is effectively out of control.

  _____

  b The problem is everyone's responsibility. The public blame the government for it.

  _____

  c The cause of the problem is the lack of basic training. The cause is not immediately obvious to everyone.

  _____

  d The solution is, in my opinion, by far the best. The solution is to have a day at work where people do not use computers or other machines.

  _____

  e Office technology is the cause of much frustration at work. It requires only basic training to use.

  _____

8 Complete the sentences below so that they reflect your experience.

  1 Technology such as ..., which helps people ..., is ...

  2 People like using systems that ...

  3 I like devices which ...

  4 People in my country use ..., which ...

Unit 3

Expressing result and purpose

1 Think of your own experiences and list at least three skills that you have learnt in the past year.

2 The extract below contains three paragraphs, each organized to express functions such as cause and result. Identify the ideas that relate to each function and underline them. The first paragraph has been done for you.

First of all, in recent years, many people all over the world have demonstrated <u>a clear lack of ability to carry out certain basic tasks</u>. A number of reasons have been put forward for this, but by far the most important, I feel, is <u>the complexity of the modern age</u>.

Parents, for example, no longer have enough time to spend at home with their children, because many are working unsociable hours to cope with the pressures and demands of today's world. Young people are consequently deprived of valuable time to learn the practical skills necessary for everyday life, like fixing a plug, mending a puncture on a bicycle, or even sewing a button on a shirt.

Apart from parents, the international drive towards learning new technology also needs to carry a good part of the blame. This has led to young people leaving school literate in certain computer skills. But it has also created a generation almost deficient in basic practical skills, because technical problem-solving like making things in carpentry has been squeezed out of the school curriculum.

— Problem

— Cause

Paragraph 1: Problem/Cause
Paragraph 2: Example/Cause/Effect
Paragraph 3: Cause/Result 1/Result 2/Reason/Example

3 Which linking devices are used in exercise 2 to express the functions listed?

4 Decide whether the linking devices below express *result* or *purpose*.

so ■ therefore ■ in order to ■ consequently ■ so as to ■ as a result
with the aim of ■ and so ■ so that ■ for this reason ■ as a consequence
hence ■ which leads to ■ which means that

Technique

Learn at least one result phrase and one purpose phrase and use these as trigger words. When you write a sentence, insert your result/purpose trigger words to develop it.

5 For each idea below, continue the sentence or write a follow-on sentence using your own ideas to express *result* or *purpose*.

a Children are now learning how to do mental arithmetic again.

b Some cities charge motorists to take their cars into the centre.

c Machines are manufactured to break down after a certain time.

Practice Test 3

Task 1

You should spend about 20 minutes on this task.

The diagram below shows how salt is removed from sea water to make it drinkable.

Summarize the information by selecting and reporting the main features and make comparisons where relevant.

Write at least 150 words.

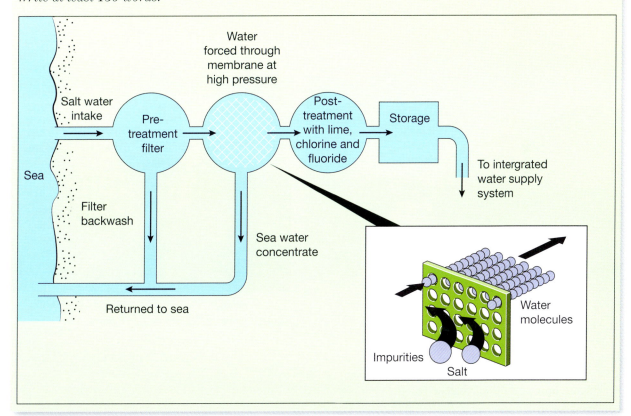

Technique

Think of a verb and/or a noun for each stage in the process:

The intake of water/take in water, filter/filtration, return, force through, remove/removal, treat/treatment, store/storage, distribute/distribution.

Task 2

You should spend about 40 minutes on this task.

Write about the following topic:

The widespread use of the Internet has brought many problems. What do you think are the main problems connected with using the web? What solutions can you suggest?

Give reasons for your answer and include any relevant examples from your own knowledge or experience.

Write at least 250 words.

Technique

Use a range of expressions to introduce effects: *leads to, results in, causes something to happen, has a big/significant impact on, plays an important role in (+ ing).*

UNIT AIMS

TASK 1 Using general and specific statements
Paraphrasing
Describing proportions

TASK 2 Avoiding overgeneralization
Developing reasons

Task 1 Using general and specific statements

1 Decide which university building below is more attractive. Which of these two universities would you prefer to go to?

2 The statements below give students' reasons for choosing a particular university. Which of these statements do you agree with?

a The lecturers' qualifications are more important than the quality of the teaching.

b The sports facilities are as important as the academic resources.

c Good library facilities are the most important factor for postgraduate students.

d A pleasant environment is more important than the university's reputation.

3 Look at the pie charts and the Task 1 question. Answer questions a–f on page 31.

Task 1

The pie charts illustrate the number of journal articles read per week by all students, PhD students and junior lecturers at an Australian university.

Summarize the information by selecting and reporting the main features, and make comparisons where relevant.

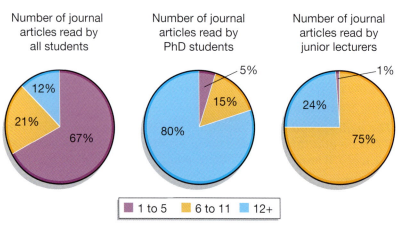

Number of journal articles read by all students

Number of journal articles read by PhD students

Number of journal articles read by junior lecturers

■ 1 to 5 ■ 6 to 11 ■ 12+

a   What does each pie chart describe?
b   What do the numbers on each pie chart represent?
c   What does the box at the bottom of the pie charts refer to?
d   What noticeable feature can you see in each chart?
e   What general statements can you make about each chart?
f   Where in your answer can you put the general overview of all the charts?

4 Complete sentences a–g using the phrases below.

> that ■ respectively ■ for example ■ how ■ but ■ which ■ meanwhile ■ whereas ■ and

a   The three pie charts illustrate _____ many articles from academic journals are read weekly by PhD students _____ junior lecturers compared to other students at an Australian university.

b   _____ , the overwhelming majority of those studying doctorates read at least twelve articles per week in comparison with the average student.

c   The figures were 80 per cent and 12 per cent _____ .

d   Furthermore, only five per cent of PhD level students read between one and five articles, _____ the average for all students in this category is a hefty 67 per cent.

e   _____ , for junior lecturers the pattern appears to be slightly different.

f   Most read six or more articles per week (99 per cent), _____ out of this total 24 per cent read 12 or more, _____ is almost a third of the corresponding figure for PhD level students.

g   It is clear _____ those students who are researching for a PhD read more articles than either junior lecturers or other students.

5 Underline 5–7 words and phrases from the sentences in exercise 4 that you think will be useful to remember, e.g. *it is clear that.* What synonyms do you know for these words and phrases?

6 The sentences in exercise 4 form a model text. Group the sentences into four paragraphs.

Paragraph 1 Introduction: _____   Paragraph 3 Body: _____

Paragraph 2 Body: _____   Paragraph 4 Conclusion/Overview: _____

7 Descriptions contain general and specific statements. Specific statements contain reference to data, whereas general statements do not. Which statements in exercise 4 are general? Which are specific?

8 Divide the following sentences into general and specific statements.

Examples

General: *Postgraduate students tended to be better off than other students.*

Specific: *75 per cent of schoolchildren read comics each week.*

a   Far fewer female lecturers than male lecturers are employed at the University, 25 and 75 respectively.
b   We can see that there are considerable differences in the proportion of nationalities in each course.
c   Only ten per cent of postgraduate students attended taught classes.
d   Overall, women were more likely to read novels than men.
e   Students preparing for their doctorate read the greatest number of journal articles.
f   The sales for all four companies showed similar trends.
g   The pattern for senior lecturers was very different.
h   The vast majority of those students preparing for PhDs read 12 or more journal articles each week.

9 Write sentences using the notes below.

1 clear/differences/pattern/student/enrolment/university/in/different years
2 less/one third/children/rural areas/obtain place/university
3 greater/number/boys/choose/study/physics/girls
4 international students/make up/21 per cent/total/number/university
5 clear/relationship/parental income/children/achievement/school exams

Paraphrasing

1 Rewrite the following sentences using the given words in brackets so that the meaning is the same.

a Far more PhD students read over 12 articles a week compared with junior lecturers. (Far fewer)
b The average student reads fewer journal articles than the average junior lecturer. (The average junior lecturer)
c The other students at the university do not read as many articles as the average PhD student. (The average PhD student)
d Junior lecturers do not have as much time to read articles as those students who are researching for a PhD. (Those students who are researching for a PhD)

Describing proportions

1 Decide which proportions the sections in blue represent:

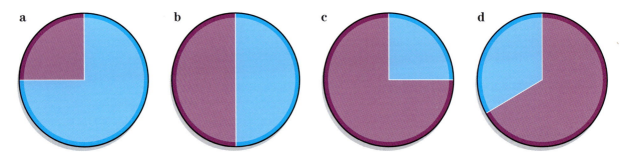

a   b   c   d

2 The phrases in the list are alternative ways of describing proportions. Divide the list into four groups that each have similar meanings.

three quarters ■ almost half ■ one third ■ 75 per cent ■ one in three ■ nearly half ■ 26 per cent
48 per cent ■ about one in four ■ 33 per cent ■ three out of four ■ just under one half
just over a quarter ■ close to one half

3 These adjective-noun collocations can also be used to describe proportions. Write the adjectives next to the correct meaning in the table.

the *vast* majority ■ a *tiny* minority ■ a *massive* 85 per cent ■ a *modest* twelve per cent
a *hefty* 85 per cent ■ a *mere* twelve per cent ■ the *overwhelming* majority

very big	
very big (used before numbers)	
very small	
not very big (used before numbers)	

4 Rewrite sentences a–e, replacing the phrases in italics with an alternative expression.

> **Technique**
>
> Vary the way you express proportions – sometimes use words instead of numbers.

  a We see from the chart that *23 per cent of* students failed to finish their university degree.

  b In 1990, *nine out of ten* engineering students were male, but by 2000 this figure had fallen to *exactly three quarters*.

  c In 1960, *34 per cent* of science graduates went into the teaching profession but in 1970, the figure was just *10 per cent*.

  d *Exactly one half* of the student population were members of the union in 2001, but five years later the figure was *64 per cent*.

  e *92 per cent* of people surveyed felt that mixed sex schools were preferable.

5 Read the Task 1 question below and answer questions a–d.

Task 1

The pie charts show the number of hours spent in a British university library by undergraduates, postgraduates and the total student population.

Summarize the information by selecting and reporting the main features and make comparisons where relevant.

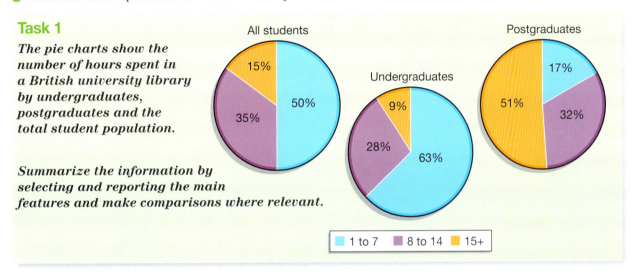

  a What are the similarities between postgraduate and all students?
  b What are the main differences between undergraduate and postgraduate students?
  c What tendency can you observe as students move from undergraduate to postgraduate?
  d What general conclusions can you draw?

6 Choose the most suitable alternative to complete the sentences below about the data in exercise 5.

  a Meanwhile, the *pattern/amount/majority* for postgraduate students was substantially different.

  b Overall, the *pattern/size/proportion* of postgraduate students who spent fifteen hours a week or more in the library was very close to the entire student body who spent 1–7 hours in the library.

  c The most striking difference in the data for undergraduates was that a sizeable *majority/minority/number* spent only 1–7 hours per week in the library.

  d A *majority/minority/total* of undergraduates (nine per cent) used the library for fifteen or more hours per week.

  e There is a clear *trend/progress/drift* towards using the library more as students move towards graduation and post-graduation.

  f Undergraduate students were less likely than postgraduate students to use the library with just under *one quarter/one third/two-thirds* of the first group spending 1–7 hours there.

  g About a *third/quarter/minority* of undergraduate students as opposed to nearly a third of postgraduate students spent between eight and fourteen hours studying.

7 In your own words, write two sentences about each pie chart and one summarizing sentence.

Task 2   Avoiding overgeneralization

1 Read the sentences below. Then answer questions a–c.

■ The international community should ensure that education is free for all schoolchildren.
■ They should provide books.
■ Parents should be encouraged to become involved in schools.

a How are the ideas connected?
b Do the second and third sentences support the first sentence?
c What ideas can you think of to support the first sentence?

2 The opinion statement below is very broad. In your opinion, which reason is most appropriate?

Opinion statement: Education is a major factor in lifting people out of poverty

Reason 1: … since it gives people more ideas about what to do with their lives.

Reason 2: … because it gives them greater opportunities when they look for work.

> **Technique**
>
> Avoid overgeneralizing by giving reasons. A common criticism of IELTS candidates is that they overgeneralize in Task 2.

3 For each statement below, decide whether you agree or disagree.

a Universities should make more links with businesses.
b The present young generation knows more than previous ones.
c Teaching thinking at school is essential, even at primary level.
d More time needs to be spent learning music, either during or after school hours.
e Physical education is a necessary part of the learning process for all pupils.
f Play is a major part of the learning process for children.
g It is important for children to try to learn another language early in their education.
h Being bored and learning to deal with boredom is a necessary part of the learning process for children.

4 Look again at the statements you agreed with in exercise 3. Do you think they are general or specific? Do they need more information like reasons and examples to make them clearer?
Give reasons for your choice.

5 Choose phrases below to intensify your opinions in exercise 3.

Example
It is important that *universities should make more links with business.*

> It is important that ■ There is no doubt that ■ One cannot deny that
> It is impossible to argue against the fact that ■ There is no denying that
> It is undeniable that

6 Look again at the phrases you disagreed with in exercise 3. It is possible to present opinions as belonging to someone else. Choose from the phrases below and add these to the sentences you disagreed with in exercise 4.

> Some people think/feel/believe/claim/argue that ■ Other people are of the opinion that
> Yet other people put forward the view that

Technique

Make sure you justify an opinion with a reason when using a general statement. Use phrases such as *because* and *since* as trigger words.

7 To avoid overgeneralization, give reasons. Add the reasons below to opinions a–h in exercise 3.

1 *since* it creates a healthy basis for later life.

2 *as* it helps the brain to function better and increases coordination.

3 *because* children now find it more difficult to reason.

4 *since* they have more access to information.

5 *because* it helps them intellectually and also helps them to find a job.

6 *as* this would connect their research with the real world.

7 *because* interaction helps to develop social skills.

8 *as* it teaches them how to be creative on their own.

Developing reasons

1 In the IELTS exam, opinions and reasons should be supported with 'examples from your knowledge and experience'. Sentences a–c give three examples to support the argument below. Match each example with the descriptions 1–3.

Play is a major part of the learning process for children as it teaches them how to be creative.

a Take, for example, children in my country who learn musical games at an early age.

b For instance, children who draw and paint are widely known to be better coordinated.

c For example, play can develop artistic or musical skills.

1 a general example

2 an example from knowledge

3 an example from experience

2 Develop the ideas below by adding your own examples like those in exercise 1.

> For instance, ■ For example, ■ like ■ namely ■ Take, for example, ■ A good example is

a Out of school activities help children develop because they can learn subjects that are not in the school curriculum.

b The focus in education is on grades rather than on learning.

c Travel helps to broaden the minds of children because it helps to bring to life the things they read in class.

d Private education goes very well with state education as it can do things state education cannot.

e Successful entrepreneurs and sports stars should teach in schools and universities since they would provide good role models for young people.

3 Develop three of the sentences below. Use phrases to intensify your own or others' opinions. Give your own reasons and examples.

Example
Too much emphasis is put on passing exams.

> *Some people feel that* too much emphasis is put on passing exams, *because* pupils spend a large proportion of school time doing tests rather than learning. *For example,* children in some British schools prepare for tests for weeks before the exams, *but* they are not taught anything.

Technique

Illustrate any reasons that you state with examples. Use phrases such as *For example/For instance* and *such as/like* as trigger words.

a Foreign language learning should be compulsory.

b Students need to have good study skills on entering university.

c University lecturers need some teacher training.

d Boys and girls ought to be educated in separate schools.

e Teachers' salaries need to be as high as doctors' or lawyers'.

Practice Test 4

Task 1

You should spend about 20 minutes on this task.

The bar chart shows the percentage of people in the United Kingdom per age group without any qualifications.

Summarize the information by selecting and reporting the main features and make comparisons where relevant.

Write at least 150 words.

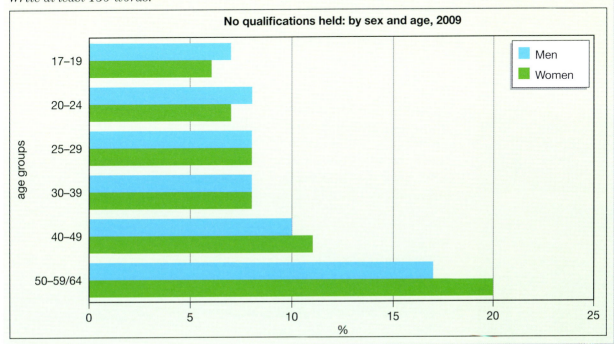

Task 2

You should spend about 40 minutes on this task.

Write about the following topic:

Some people believe that competitive sports, both team and individual, have no place in the school curriculum. To what extent do you agree or disagree?

Give reasons for your answer and include any relevant examples from your own knowledge or experience.

Write at least 250 words.

Checklist

1 Decide which side you generally agree with.

2 Write an introduction of two sentences to develop the general topic of the question.

3 Use trigger words like *for example* and *because* to give some possible reasons. Do this for both sides of the argument (possible reasons why competitive sports do and don't have a place).

4 Write three main paragraphs, one for the opinion that you disagree with and two for your own opinion. Give a reason in each one and, if you can, an example.

5 Write a conclusion of one or two sentences summarizing your opinion and giving your main reasons.

5 Youth

a

Task 1 Describing changes

1 Match the photos a–c to the comments by three people talking about the town where they grew up.

> **Dave**
>
> I remember there wasn't much to do here when I was growing up. My friends and I used to just hang around in the park, getting into trouble. These days there's much more here for young people. For instance, *the council opened the ice rink, the leisure centre and the skate park last year*. I wish I'd had things like that to keep me entertained.

b

> **Sandra**
>
> One of the things I used to really like about this area was the peace and quiet. It was so safe for us as kids. We could play in the streets or in the nearby woods and fields. *They built a bypass and an industrial estate a few years ago* and there's been a lot more traffic and development since. I don't feel it's safe for my children and I'd like to move away.

> **Tom**
>
> Well, you can't stand in the way of change, I suppose. Yes, people look at the town now with lots of shiny tower blocks and say it's not as pretty or peaceful as it was in the past. Even so, there are more jobs and opportunities now than there were when I was a teenager.

c

2 Read the comments above again. Answer the questions below.

a For each speaker, do they think things were better or worse when they were young? Why?

b What changes have occurred in the place you come from? Do you think they are positive or negative changes?

c How could you express the phrases in italics in a more formal way?

d Imagine you are a young person moving to a new town. Which facilities in the list below would be important to you?

> golf course ▪ skate park ▪ theatre ▪ railway station ▪ concert hall ▪ gallery
> stadium ▪ ice rink ▪ park ▪ college ▪ airport

3 The maps below show changes that took place in Youngsville in New Zealand over a 20-year period from 1990 to 2010. Answer the following questions:

a What is the most noticeable difference between the two maps?
b Was the town more or less residential in 2010 compared to 1990?
c Were there more or fewer trees in 2010?
d Were the changes dramatic or slight over the 20-year period?
e What were the two biggest changes north of the river?
f What happened to the houses and trees along the railway line south of the river?

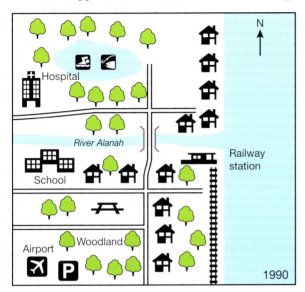

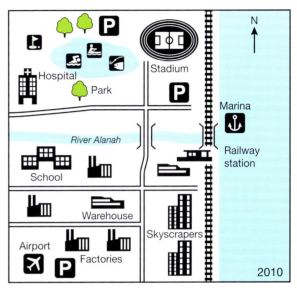

4 Complete the text below. Use one word from the following list to complete each blank space. The first one has been done for you.

houses ■ experienced ■ noticeable ■ factories ■ developments ■ comparison
residential ■ corner ■ facilities ■ construction

The maps show the **1** _developments_ which took place in the coastal town of Youngsville between 1990 and 2010.
In 1990, the town was a much greener **2** _____ area with a large number of trees and individual houses, but during the next 20 years the town **3** _____ a number of dramatic changes. The most **4** _____ is that all of the trees south of the River Alanah were cut down, with all the **5** _____ along the railway line being knocked down and replaced by skyscrapers. Moreover, a new industrial estate with **6** _____ and warehouses sprang up around the airport and school.
Only a few trees north of the river remained. The woodland was cleared to make way for a park, a golf course and car parking **7** _____ . Further developments were the **8** _____ of a stadium near the north-east **9** _____ of the lake and a new stretch of railway from the river running directly north. A marina was also built at the mouth of the river.
Overall, a **10** _____ of the two maps reveals a change from a largely rural to a mainly urban landscape.

Technique

Identify changes in the maps and number them on the second one. Think of some general statements and make notes. Remember to write an overview.

5 Answer the questions below about the text in exercise 4.

1 What information is given in the introductory paragraph?

_____

2 Which sentence in paragraph two gives an overview of the changes?

_____

3 Which part of the map does the rest of paragraph two describe?

_____

4 Which part of the map is described in paragraph three?

_____

5 In paragraph three does the description move west to east, or east to west?

_____

6 Which two adjectives in the conclusion sum up the changes?

_____

6 Transform the sentences below by changing the nouns into verbs and by using the passive. Refer to page 7 for more information on using nouns to summarize.

Example
There were *spectacular changes* in the area. The area *was changed* spectacularly.

Technique
Do not just describe the map or maps. Describe the developments that took place.

a There were dramatic developments in the town centre.

_____

b There was a complete transformation of the neighbourhood.

_____

c There was a total reconstruction of the residential area.

_____

d There was a total redevelopment of the old factories.

_____

e There was a rebuilding of the old houses.

_____

f There was a complete modernization of the entertainment district.

_____

7 Look again at the sentences you wrote in exercise 6. Which could be rewritten in the active form?

8 Rewrite sentences a–h below using synonyms from the text in exercise 4.
a The maps show changes which *occurred* between 1990 and 2010.
b Very few trees *were left*.
c Over the next 25 years, all these houses *were demolished*.
d The houses *were replaced* by skyscrapers.
e The trees *were chopped down*.
f The area *witnessed* dramatic changes.
g The woodland *gave way* to a golf course.
h A marina *was also constructed*.

9 Put the verbs below into the correct form. All of the changes took place between 2005 and 2012.

Examples

The block of flats _____*was turned*_____ (turn) into a hotel. (passive)

The block of flats _____*made way*_____ (make way) for a hotel. (active)

a The row of old houses _____ (knock down) to make way for a road.

b The forest _____ (cut down) to build a railway.

c The area _____ (redevelop) completely.

d The factory _____ (convert) into an art gallery.

e The city centre _____ (undergo) a total transformation.

f The row of old terraced houses in the city _____ (pull down) and _____ (replace) by a block of flats.

g A sports complex _____ (construct) in the suburbs.

h A number of spectacular changes _____ (take place).

i The whole centre of the town _____ (transform) by new developments.

10 Which of the following cannot be used to replace the phrase *Between 2005 and 2012*?

a Over the period

b During the seven-year period

c From 2005 to 2012

d Over the past seven years

11 Insert *By 2012* at the beginning of each sentence in exercise 9 and adjust each sentence. Use the Technique box to help you.

> ## Technique
> Use the past perfect (had done) to describe changes occurring before a specific time in the past, e.g. *By 2012, the block of flats had been turned into a hotel* (passive). *By 2012, the block of flats had made way* for a hotel (active).

Describing locations

1 Answer the questions a–g about the maps on page 39 using the phrases in the box.

> south of the river ■ in the south-west of the town ■ north of the skyscrapers
> to the south of the golf course ■ south west of the stadium ■ in the north-east of the town
> just to the north of the river mouth

a Where is the lake? It is _____ .

b Where is the hospital? It is _____ .

c Where is the railway station? It is _____ .

d Where is the airport? It is _____ .

e Where is the school? It is _____ .

f Where is the stadium? It is _____ .

g Where is the marina? It is _____ .

> ## Technique
> State locations clearly on a map. Sometimes we can do this by referring to their position on the whole area shown. In this case, we say *in the north/south/west/east of* …We can also talk about the position of an item in relation to other items on the map. In this case, we say *north/south of* with no preposition or *to the north/south of*. Look at the examples.
>
> ### *Examples*
> The airport is *in the south-west of the town*.
> Only a few trees (to the) *north of the river* remained.
> Where is the golf course? It is (to the) *north-west of the lake*.

2 Complete the following sentences by choosing the correct prepositions of place from the alternatives.

   a Several changes took place *at/in/on* the town of Northgate.

   b North of the town, there is a lake surrounded *in/of/by* trees.

   c A number of new houses were built *beside/at/on* the railway line.

   d There was a large industrial area located *on/in/at* the north.

   e A new railway was constructed which ran *from/at/in* north to south.

   f Two new hotels were erected *on/in/at* the banks of the river.

   g A large number of new villas were built *beside/at/to* the sea.

   h A yachting club was set up *on/in/at* the shores of the lake.

   i A number of wind turbines were placed in the sea, just *off/on/to* the coastline.

3 Choose five prepositional phrases of place from the sentences in exercise 2 to record.
   Example
   in the town

Task 2 Developing and justifying opinions

1 Look at the photo and the speech bubbles. Answer the questions below.
   a Which person do you agree with?
   b Do you agree with the justification for each person's opinion?
   c Is this situation the same all over the world?

2 Read the following Task 2 question and then answer questions a–b.

> *Employers should pay young people the same salary as older colleagues doing the same job.*
> *To what extent do you agree or disagree?*

   a Do you have to strongly agree or disagree? Is it possible to take a neutral view?
   b Rewrite the statement in your own words. Begin with *Young employees …*

3 Read a–g, taken from an answer to the question in exercise 2. Match each sentence or part-sentence with the correct function from the list. The first one has been done for you.

> Contradiction ▪ Explanation ▪ Result ▪ Example ▪ Reason (x 2) ▪ ~~Opinion statement~~

a Many people believe that workers should be paid according to age rather than merit.

Opinion statement

b However, I feel that they should be paid according to results.

_____

c Take, for example, someone in their twenties working in a financial company.

_____

d They deserve to receive the same salary …

_____

e … because they are doing the same work.

_____

f Moreover, young people nowadays are often faster at doing things than their older work colleagues …

_____

g … which compensates for lack of experience.

_____

4 Underline the linking devices in exercise 3 which indicate the functions you chose.

5 Using the sentences in exercise 3 as a model, write a paragraph expressing your own opinion in response to the question in 2. Use appropriate linking devices.

6 Read the Task 2 question and the extract below. For each of 1–6, two options are possible and one is incorrect. Delete the incorrect option.

> *Some people feel that young people face more pressures today than in previous generations. Others think that they have a much easier life than their parents did. What is your opinion?*

Life for the young in today's world is in some ways certainly more comfortable than for those in previous generations. **1** *However/Moreover/Even so*, one cannot deny the fact that in a number of areas life is much more demanding than it used to be.

Take the workplace, for example. Competition for every job is now fierce in all parts of the world, not just developed countries, **2** *while/because/as* young people are more qualified than previous generations. **3** *Furthermore/Likewise/And*, there is increased mobility of people in the international job market. Skilled workers move from the Far East to Europe. India, **4** *for instance/also/in particular*, has a large pool of mobile skilled workers. This globalization of jobs has **5** *consequently/however/as a result* put intense pressure on young people as they search for work in their home countries. **6** *Thus/So/Subsequently*, it is no longer a case of just being good; young people are expected to be top rate.

7 Decide which functions are indicated by the correct linking devices in exercise 6.

1	**a** contrast	**b** result	**c** addition
2	**a** contrast	**b** reason	**c** result
3	**a** addition	**b** contrast	**c** result
4	**a** contrast	**b** addition	**c** example
5	**a** result	**b** contrast	**c** reason
6	**a** example	**b** reason	**c** conclusion

8 Read the statements below and in each case contradict them. Begin by using one of the following expressions in the box.

> Nevertheless, I feel … ■ However, I think … ■ Personally, I believe …

a Many feel that young people today have much more influence in the world than past generations.

_____

b According to some people, older workers are just as equipped to deal with the modern world as young people.

_____

c Some people feel that modern advertising encourages a negative view of older people and older workers.

_____

> **Technique**
> Always develop and justify opinions. Make a statement and use linking devices as trigger words to think up and organize ideas.

Writing introductions

1 Read the questions and introductions below. Match each introduction a–c with one of the questions 1–4.

1 All forms of media but especially films and TV programmes should be censored to protect young people. To what extent do you agree?

2 The younger generation are the main driving force behind many of the latest technological developments. How far do you agree?

3 Blogs on the web are very effective ways for people to express their ideas. What is your opinion?

4 The modern emphasis on computers reduces the development of any creative ability. How far do you agree?

a It is certainly important to make sure that people are protected from harmful material in various media. However, I feel that care needs to be taken in doing so for various reasons.

b In some areas, it does appear that computers reduce creativity, but I also feel they can be used as a tool to develop creative ability in many fields.

c While the youth of today definitely have an impact on the way new technology develops, there are other factors involved.

> **Technique**
> Keep your introductions short. Write only one or two sentences.

2 For the remaining title, write your own introduction. Try to paraphrase the statement in the title in one sentence. Then write another statement to show how you intend to organize your essay using a general noun.

Practice Test 5

Task 1

You should spend about 20 minutes on this task.

The maps below show the changes that took place at the seaside resort of Templeton between 2000 and 2013.

Summarize the information by selecting and reporting the main features and make comparisons where relevant.

Write at least 150 words.

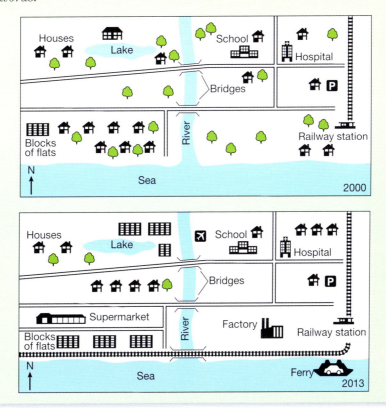

Task 1 Checklist

1 Look at the information on the maps and note any dates given.

2 Paraphrase the task statement in the introduction.

3 Write an overview sentence to summarize the types of changes.

4 Decide on a way to organize your answer, e.g. changes in the north and changes in the south.

5 Write two paragraphs about the details of the changes.

6 Write a concluding paragraph summarizing the changes, if necessary.

Task 2

You should spend about 40 minutes on this task. Write about the following topic:

Young people are much more aware of and concerned about issues like the environment, poverty and animal welfare than previous generations. What is your own opinion?

Give reasons for your answer and include any relevant examples from your own knowledge or experience.

Write at least 250 words.

UNIT AIMS

TASK 1 Writing overviews
Describing two sets of data
Using complex sentences:
Concession (1)

TASK 2 Expressing advantages and
disadvantages
Using advantage and disadvantage
vocabulary
Using complex sentences:
Concession (2)

Task 1 Writing overviews

1 Give at least three advantages of each cultural activity shown in the pictures.

2 Rank the activities in the list below 1–10 according to how important they are in developing understanding between different cultures (1 = most important; 10 = least important).

organizing student exchanges _____

language learning _____

setting up international trade agreements _____

advertising similar climate and landscape _____

creating joint cultural events _____

establishing transport links _____

promoting tourism _____

sharing scientific and technological know-how _____

promoting positive media images _____

highlighting similarities in lifestyle and culture _____

3 Think of examples to justify your choices in exercise 2. Are there any activities that might be difficult to develop or promote?

4 Which of the activities in exercise 2 can be carried out by individuals? Which can be carried out by governments?

5 Statements a–c were used to write overviews of data. Put the words in italics in the correct order.

a It is clear that *majority/people/overwhelming/of/the/were/of/favour/in* school visits between countries.

_____

b Overall, just over half the people surveyed found the climate in the tropics the most difficult thing to adapt to, *a/number/with/smaller/naming/and/lifestyle/food*.

_____

c The three languages in question, Spanish, Arabic and Chinese, were named as *important/the/languages/most/after English by about/of/equal/people/numbers*.

_____

Technique

Write an overview for every Task 1 question. This will help you to achieve a good score. You can place the overview just after the introduction, in the first sentence of the second paragraph or as a separate short paragraph at the end like a conclusion.

6 Answer these questions about the sentences in exercise 5 on page 46.

    a Which activity in exercise 2 do they relate to?

    b Which pie chart 1–4 below would be a good illustration of each statement in exercise 5? Use the proportions in each sentence to help you.

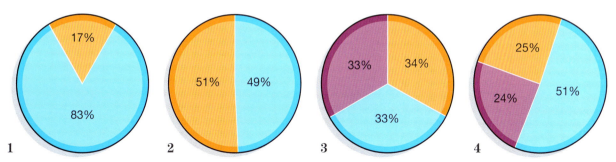

1   2   3   4

7 Pie charts are frequently used to summarize data. Match each of the following overviews to one of the pie charts 1–4 above.

    a To conclude, only a small minority of people felt that the language barrier would prevent the development of cultural links.

    b It is evident that opinions are split almost equally between the three options as regards the benefits of joint cultural ventures.

    c It would seem that the vast majority of people think that the development of trade links has the greatest impact on international relations.

    d Just under half the people surveyed are of the opinion that China would be the biggest cultural influence in the world by 2020.

    e About half of the holiday makers visited Italy because they were interested in the art and culture, whereas the food and the climate were named as the most important factors by approximately equal numbers of the remaining tourists in the survey.

> ### Technique
>
> Aim to include several key features in your Task 1 answer: a paraphrase of the question, proportion phrases, comparisons, some general and some specific statements/clauses about the data, along with an overview.

8 Rewrite the sentences below using a suitable phrase from the list.

> nearly a third ▪ almost equal numbers ▪ the vast majority
> a tiny minority ▪ just under half ▪ ~~nearly two-thirds~~

Examples

Government subsidies accounted for *63 per cent of all funding*.
Government subsidies accounted for *nearly two-thirds of all funding*.

    a *87 per cent of holiday makers* to China were very satisfied with their experience.

    b It is clear that *about 50 per cent of both sexes* favoured increased cultural contacts.

    c Only *11 per cent of filmgoers* thought films helped promote cultural awareness.

    d In conclusion, the trend is clearly upward, with *47 per cent of companies* establishing new trade and cultural links in 2012.

    e To sum up, *32 per cent of all tourists* were on some form of package holiday.

9 Look again at the sentences in exercises 5, 6 and 8. Make a list of phrases which are used to indicate overviews.

Describing two sets of data

1 Study Task 1 below and answer questions a–c.

> **The table below shows the age profile of tourists on backpacking holidays and guided tours in New Zealand in 2012 and the pie chart gives the satisfaction rating of their stay. Summarize the information by selecting and reporting the main features and make comparisons where relevant.**

Age profile	Backpacking	Guided tours
18–30	62%	7%
31–40	23%	22%
41–50	10%	57%
Other	5%	14%

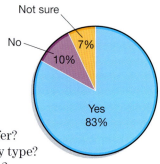

a How does the age profile of people on each type of holiday differ?
b Which age group is almost equally represented on each holiday type?
c How would you describe the opinion of the majority of visitors?

2 Complete the text with verbs from the box. The first one has been done for you.

> comes ■ accounts for ■ belong ■ ~~provides~~ ■ enjoyed ■ is rated ■ make up ■ include

The table **1** _provides_ a breakdown by selected age group of those on backpacking and guided tours in New Zealand in 2012, with the pie chart indicating whether they **2** _____ their holiday.
As can be seen from the table, the age profile of people on the two different types of holiday varies considerably. For example, the majority (62 per cent) of those on backpacking holidays **3** _____ to the 18–30 age range, but the same age group **4** _____ a small proportion (seven per cent) of those on guided tours. However, the pattern is the complete reverse when it **5** _____ to 41–50 year-olds. These people **6** _____ 57 per cent of those on guided tours, despite accounting for only ten per cent of backpackers.
By contrast, the profiles for both backpacking and guided tours **7** _____ roughly equal proportions from the 31–40 age group: 23 and 22 per cent respectively.
It is clear from the pie chart that New Zealand **8** _____ as a popular holiday destination among the majority of all holiday makers, with a massive 83 per cent from both groups stating they enjoyed their holiday.

3 Which phrases and sentences in the text in exercise 2 indicate:
a a phrase directing attention to the table
b a phrase summarizing the data in the table
c a general sentence about 41–50 year-olds
d an overview about the satisfaction rating

> **Technique**
> Use a variety of verbs such as *form*, *make up*, *account for* when you describe proportions.

4 Using your own words, write a paraphrase of the phrases and sentences in exercise 3.

> **Technique**
> Show that you can combine ideas in complex sentences.

Using complex sentences: Concession (1)

1 Read the example sentences below then answer questions a–c.

Examples
57 per cent of people on guided tours were aged 41–50, although only 10 per cent of backpackers belonged to this age group.
57 per cent of people on guided tours were aged 41–50. Nevertheless, only 10 per cent of backpackers belonged to this age group.

  a Which linking devices are used to introduce a contrast?
  b How are the devices used differently?
  c Find three examples of similar devices in the text in exercise 2 on page 48. Which devices in the example sentences are they like? Which device can only be used before a noun or an *-ing* form?

2 Match a–e below with suitable sentences or sentence endings 1–5 to create correct statements about the data in exercise 1 on page 48.

  a *Despite* accounting for nearly equal proportions of each holiday type,
  b *Although* people aged 41–50 were dominant on guided tours,
  c Guided tours were least popular among people in the 18–30 age group,
  d One in ten people said that they didn't enjoy their holiday.
  e Only 14 per cent of people from the four other categories chose guided tours.

  1 they still accounted for one in ten backpackers.
  2 *Nevertheless*, most clearly expressed satisfaction.
  3 this age group still accounted for under a quarter of each.
  4 *However*, that was still a higher proportion than the 18–30 age group.
  5 *but* they were most popular with the oldest group.

3 Join each of the following sentences using the phrase given.

  a The vast majority of visitors to Britain come from Europe. However, they stay for fewer than ten days on average.
    Although _____ _____

  b 45 per cent of people speak a foreign language. Nevertheless, the vast majority are at a low level.
    Although 45 per cent _____

  c It has good weather. However, southern France is visited by only two per cent of Asian tourists.
    Despite _____

  d The cost of student exchanges went up. Nevertheless, the number of exchanges rose.
    The number of student exchanges _____

  e The event was promoted to teenagers. Nevertheless, they accounted for only 32 per cent of the audience.
    Although _____

4 Look at the table below which gives information about three cinemas. Write five sentences about the information using the concession words in exercises 2 and 3.

	Number of screens	Number of admissions 2012	Revenue 2012
Plaza	3	510,957	$ 2,759,167
Cinelink	2	523,899	$ 2,758,943
Roxy	5	763,902	$ 2,812,400

Task 2 Expressing advantages and disadvantages

1 Look at the photos of popular electronic items. Which ideas in the box explain the popularity of each item in the pictures? What do you think the next electronic craze will be?

> size ■ design ■ portability ■ technology
> business need ■ entertainment ■ fashion ■ price

2 Read the Task 2 question below. Then answer the questions.

Task 2

Portable entertainment devices, such as MP3 or DVD players, which allow people to listen to music or watch films on the move, are now commonplace. What do you think are the main advantages and disadvantages of this development?

Give reasons for your answer and include any relevant examples from your own knowledge or experience.

    a Which part of the question states the general subject?
    b Which part of the question contains the general nouns to help you organize your answer?

3 Decide whether each idea below is an advantage or a disadvantage. Which entertainment devices would you associate them with?

    a It helps people to relax.
    b It allows people greater freedom.
    c It reduces communication.
    d It makes life more enjoyable.
    e It makes entertainment more accessible everywhere.
    f It makes people more isolated.
    g It is a nuisance for other travellers.
    h It makes people less sociable.

4 Complete each sentence a–f with a word from the box.

> help ■ difficult ■ interfere ■ benefits ■ ideal ■ enable

    a These devices bring a number of _____ .

    b The main one, in my opinion, is that they _____ people relax, for example, while they are studying or working in cafés or on trains.

    c Some people find it _____ to do so when it is completely quiet outside their homes.

    d So these devices _____ people to relax and create a familiar environment.

    e Sometimes, however, they do _____ with others if the volume is too high, hence the quiet zones in many trains.

    f Nevertheless, laptops, etc are _____ because they allow people to do things where they want to rather than being restricted to working at home.

Technique

Keep an electronic list of positive and negative words that you can use to express advantages and disadvantages. Make your own revision cards.

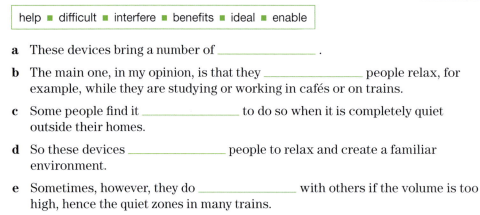

5 Decide whether the words in exercise 4 express advantage or disadvantage.

6 The sentences in exercise 4 form a paragraph taken from an answer to the Task 2 question. Answer questions a–c.

   a Which sentence in exercise 4 expresses a disadvantage?
   b Which linking devices are used in exercise 4?
   c Which ideas from exercise 3 are used in the paragraph?

7 The paragraph below is taken from a similar answer. Complete the paragraph with words from the box.

> even if ■ likewise ■ for example ■ though ■ consequently ■ and ■ although

> The main drawback is, in my opinion, quite obvious. Take, **1** _____ , people of all ages who are travelling on trains nowadays. **2** _____ they are reading, they are plugged into the radio, talking on their mobiles, or listening to music on their MP3 players. **3** _____ others are playing games, watching a film and working simultaneously, even **4** _____ they have friends next to them to talk to. **5** _____ this allows people greater freedom and flexibility **6** _____ takes away the boredom of the journeys, people are becoming more and more isolated in their own worlds. **7** _____ the art of communication is being lost.

8 Answer these questions about the paragraph in exercise 7.

   a Does this paragraph concentrate on advantages or disadvantages?
   b Which ideas does this paragraph mention from the list in exercise 3 on page 50?
   c Underline the main advantage and disadvantage in the paragraph.

Using advantage and disadvantage vocabulary

1 Nouns can be used to express advantage and disadvantage. Complete sentences a–g with words from the box.

> benefit ■ problems ■ opportunities ■ chance ■ handicap ■ drawbacks ■ gain

   a Not knowing a foreign language has its _____ , such as when one tries to make contact with people in other countries.

   b Visiting other countries gives people the _____ to experience cultures first hand.

   c The financial _____ to any nation exceeds all other benefits.

   d If people take time to find out about the country they are travelling to, they will face fewer _____ .

   e These days, not having access to the Internet to find out what is going on is a serious _____ .

   f Cultural exchanges offer enormous _____ to the nations that are involved.

   g Being culturally aware is of great _____ in business.

2 Adjectives can also be used to emphasize advantage and disadvantage. Does the word *serious* in exercise 1e emphasize advantage or disadvantage?

3 Decide whether each adjective in the box is used to express advantage or disadvantage.

advantageous ■ beneficial ■ useful ■ worthless ■ invaluable
difficult ■ helpful ■ convenient

Advantage: ___*advantageous*___

Disadvantage: _____

> **Technique**
>
> Use nouns, verbs and adjectives, such as *benefit* and *drawback*, which express advantages and disadvantages as trigger words to help you plan.

> **Technique**
>
> Keep a record of common phrases or collocations that you can use again and again, for example *to give people a chance*, *make contact*, *face problems*.

4 Write the opposite of each of the adjectives in exercise 3.
Where possible, add or remove a prefix or suffix to create the opposite.

Example
advantageous *disadvantageous*

5 Verbs such as the ones used below can be used to indicate advantages and disadvantages. Complete the following sentences in your own words.

  a International arts festivals *encourage* _____ .

  b Lending artworks to other countries *improves* _____ .

  c Films and concerts *enhance* _____ .

  d To *enable* children to value their heritage, _____ .

  e Personal links can *benefit* _____ .

  f Ignorance of other people's traditions can *hinder* _____ .

  g To *prevent* countries falling out with each other, _____ .

Using complex sentences: Concession (2)

1 Read sentences 1 and 2 and answer the questions a and b.
  1 Although the vast majority of electronic devices are very useful, they are also highly annoying.
  2 Despite being highly annoying, the vast majority of electronic gadgets are very useful.

  a Which word introduces the concession in each case?
  b Which sentence emphasizes the advantage? Which emphasizes the disadvantage?

2 Complete sentences a–e with words from the box.

nevertheless ■ however ■ despite ■ although ■ but

  a _____ listening to music on an iPod is very pleasant, it is not as good as a live concert.

  b Documentaries are invaluable sources of knowledge. _____ , they need to be entertaining as well as informative.

  c _____ the large numbers of tourists, ancient buildings and temples are still inspiring places to visit.

  d Sculptures can make gardens and public spaces attractive. _____ , they are expensive to look after.

  e Arts exhibitions show the public artefacts they would not normally see, _____ at a price.

Practice Test 6

Task 1

You should spend about 20 minutes on this task.

The table below shows how young people in Tokyo, Japan, listened to music over the previous month. The pie chart shows a record company's international findings about whether people preferred live or recorded music.

Summarize the information by selecting and reporting the main features and make comparisons where relevant.

Write at least 150 words.

	Live music	MP3 players	Internet	CDs
Male	60 %	79 %	55 %	19 %
Female	44 %	40 %	42 %	22 %

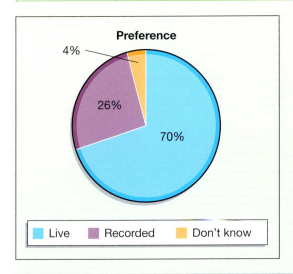

Task 2

You should spend about 40 minutes on this task. Write about the following topic:

Travellers and business people often come into contact with other cultures briefly. What are the main advantages and disadvantages of doing so?

Give reasons for your answer and include any relevant examples from your own knowledge or experience.

Write at least 250 words.

Task 2 Checklist

1 Use trigger words like *benefit* or *disadvantage* to get some ideas.

2 Write an introduction of two sentences to develop the topic of the question.

3 Choose the two most important ideas and write one or two paragraphs.

4 Develop your ideas in each paragraph using other trigger words like *because* or question words like *when*, *how* and *why*.

5 Use trigger words like *for example* to provide some examples.

6 Do the same for the disadvantages.

7 Write a conclusion summarizing the most important advantage(s) and disadvantage(s). You could also say which you think is more important.

7 Arts and sciences

UNIT AIMS

TASK 1   **Using adverbs**
            Using adverbs to evaluate data
            Avoiding irrelevance

TASK 2   **Discussing other people's opinions**
            Hypothesizing

Task 1   Using adverbs

1   Describe the cartoon and think about the meaning.

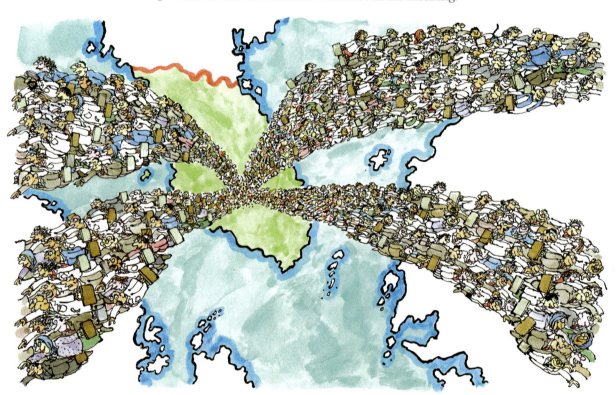

2   Read these conflicting views about scientists moving to rich countries. Answer questions a–c.

> The 'brain drain' of skilled workers like scientists and technicians to rich economies is morally wrong.

> People should have greater freedom to work where they want. Surely, it's a personal matter.

   a   Which view do you most agree with?
   b   Is this 'brain drain' a new phenomenon, or has it been around for a long time?
   c   Should something be done about the situation or is it unstoppable?

3 Read the Task 1 question below. Answer questions a–e.

Task 1

The chart shows sources of funding for research and development (R&D) in the UK from 2010 to 2012. The table below shows the percentage of national income spent on R&D for a range of countries.

Summarize the information by selecting and reporting the main features, and make comparisons where relevant.

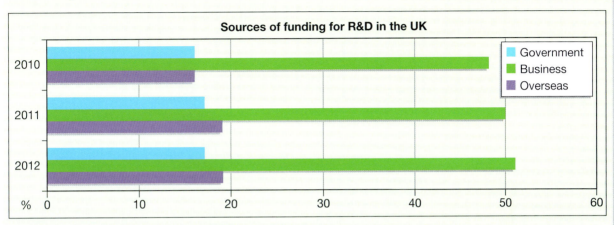

Proportion of national income allocated to R&D (2012)						
UK	**USA**	**Germany**	**France**	**Italy**	**Japan**	**EU average**
1.82%	2.75%	2.4%	2.3%	1.1%	2.9%	1.81%

a What general trend can you see in the chart?
b What general pattern can you see in the table?
c Which is clearly the main source of funding in the bar chart?
d Which piece of data in the table can you use as a standard for comparison?
e Which pieces of information in the table are significant?

4 Complete the text below with verbs from the box. The first one has been done for you.

> rose ■ contributed (x 2) ■ was ■ overtook ■ was spent ■ is shown ■ came ■ shows

The chart **1** _____*shows*_____ information about the main sources of funding for scientific research and development (R&D) in the UK. The proportion of national income spent on R&D by country **2** _____ in the table.

Between 2010 and 2012, the amount of funding allocated from each source **3** _____ very slightly. Approximately half of all investment throughout the period **4** _____ from business, while the government consistently **5** _____ around seventeen per cent. It is also noticeable that in 2010 overseas spending on R&D in the UK was comparable to the government's, at around 17 per cent. But for the last two years it **6** _____ government spending in this area.

As regards the proportion of national income allocated to R&D, the highest percentage (2.9 per cent) **7** _____ by Japan, followed closely by the USA (2.75 per cent). By contrast, Italy **8** _____ the smallest amount of national income to R&D, only 1.1 per cent, significantly below the EU average of 1.81 per cent.

It is worth noting that, although the UK's spending on R&D **9** _____ above the EU average in 2012, it is considerably behind other close trading partners France and Germany.

Technique

Use adverbs to describe adjectives and verbs. They help to make your answer clearer. Record useful collocations with verb-adverb and adverb-adjective.

5 Find examples of adverbs ending in *-ly* used in the text in exercise 4.

6 Choose the most suitable adverb in sentences a–h.

Examples

The trend for other countries was *completely/well* different.

Government investment rose *significantly/highly*.

a The government's spending for the past year was *significantly/well* higher than before.
b Women have been *consistently/deeply* under-represented in science jobs.
c Workers in *highly/lowly/considerably* paid jobs are generally healthier.
d The company's sales are *slightly/much* behind its competitors.
e Sales were *marginally/deeply* up on the previous quarter.
f Investment in the arts rose quite *considerably/slightly/seriously*.
g *Slightly/Approximately/Well* half the spending was from the private sector.
h The income for the arts centre was *substantially/much/highly* down on the previous year.

7 Match the adverbs a–g below with their opposites 1–7.

a	well	**1**	rapidly
b	marginally	**2**	slightly
c	approximately	**3**	exactly
d	constantly	**4**	badly
e	slowly	**5**	considerably
f	significantly	**6**	partially
g	completely	**7**	erratically

Using adverbs to evaluate data

1 Look again at the text in exercise 4 on page 55. Which phrases are used to introduce sentences instead of *noticeably*?

2 Rewrite each sentence a–g using an adverb or starting with *It*.

Example

Clearly, the trend is upward.

It is clear that the trend is upward.

a It is significant that the number of scientists per head of population has declined in recent years.

_____

b Obviously, the sales failed to recover.

It _____

c It is probable that numbers will continue to fall over the period.

_____

d Clearly, there were skill shortages in the chemical industry.

It _____

e Evidently, investment needs to be increased.

It _____

f Noticeably, the pattern for investment in the arts is the reverse.

It _____

g More importantly, the cost of plasma screens is set to fall.

It _____

3 Different adverbs can be put in different places in sentences. Which sentences a–d are possible?

  a *Considerably*, sales fell.
  b Sales fell *considerably*.
  c *Clearly*, the trend was downward.
  d The trend was *clearly* downward.

4 Put the adverb in brackets in the correct place in the sentence. Some can be used in more than one place.

  a The number of science graduates fell. (significantly)
  b The number of technical staff in hospitals is falling. (evidently)
  c The cost of training scientists is increasing year by year. (noticeably)
  d Investment in capital equipment like specialist machinery is down on last year. (considerably)
  e Sales of new televisions soared before the World Cup. (clearly)
  f The trend is now upward. (obviously)

5 Write your own sentences about the data in exercise 3 on page 55.

  a Describe the bar chart, using *marginally*, *approximately* and *slowly*.
  b Describe the table, using *considerably*, *evidently*, *noticeably* and *slightly*.

> **Technique**
>
> Use at least one adverb or adverbial phrase as an overview to help you evaluate the data. Put adverbs which comment on the whole idea at the beginning of the sentence. Put adverbs which only modify the verb before the main verb or after the verb *to be*.

Avoiding irrelevance

1 Look at the chart below which shows how students on all courses at an Australian university viewed different subjects on a scale of easy to difficult. Answer questions a–f.

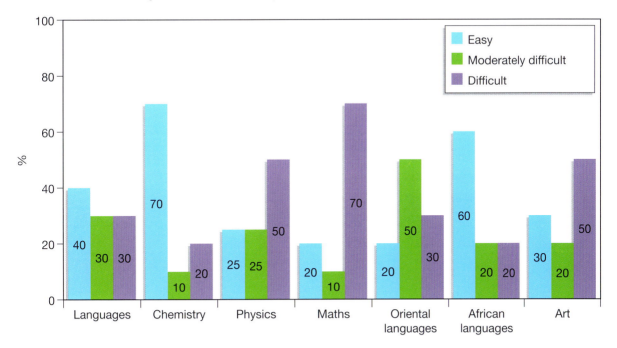

  a Whose opinions does the chart show?
  b How many subjects does the chart show?
  c Which subject was rated as 'difficult' by the highest percentage of students?
  d Which other subjects were judged 'difficult' or 'moderately difficult' by over 70 per cent of students?
  e Which subject was rated as 'easy' by the highest percentage of students?
  f Is there a clear correspondence between the type of subject and whether it was rated as easy or difficult? Give examples to show why/why not.

2 Decide whether the statements a–f are relevant or irrelevant, and explain why. Irrelevant statements may contain an unnecessary opinion, too much data or unnecessary speculation.

Technique

Do not speculate or give opinions when you describe data. Avoid going into too much detail.

a The subject which was rated as difficult by the highest percentage of students (70 per cent) was mathematics, mainly because I think it is complex for many students.

b By contrast, the subject which was most often judged as easy was chemistry.

c The chart shows the opinions of Australian students on whether different subjects were easy or difficult.

d African languages were seen as easy, which is somewhat surprising when you consider the range of languages in Africa.

e Oriental languages were ranked as easy by only about 20 per cent.

f The Y axis shows the percentages, and the bars contain the numbers about the legend at the bottom.

3 Describe the chart in exercise 1 in your own words.

Task 2 Discussing other people's opinions

1 Identify the people in the pictures.

2 Complete the list below with a famous artist and scientist from your country. Then answer the questions.

Leonardo da Vinci

Albert Einstein

Sir Isaac Newton

Nicolaus Copernicus

_____

_____

a Are the people in the list famous in your country?

b What do you know about them?

c What benefit do artists and scientists bring to society?

d Do artists and scientists in your society have a high or low status?

3 Read the Task 2 question below and say which part of the question relates to:

a People's opinions about the arts.

b People's opinions about sciences.

c Your own opinion.

a

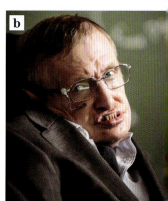

b

Some people believe that the arts should receive money from government and big companies. Others feel such spending is a luxury and that it would be better if it were invested in scientific projects.

Discuss both views and give your own opinion. Provide reasons for your answer and include any relevant examples from your own knowledge or experience.

4 Complete the paragraph with sentences a–c.

   a So supporters of arts groups feel that the company's travel and accommodation costs ought to receive more money.

   b Touring theatre groups or dance companies are a case in point.

   c Many people feel strongly that arts projects like exhibitions of photography, sculpture or paintings should be helped financially by government and big companies.

> **1** _____ They argue that such projects enrich people's lives, often simply because they are new and show a different way of doing things. **2** _____ National companies, for example, can take plays to provincial areas that don't have their own facilities. This, however, requires considerable amounts of money. **3** _____ If this were done by the government and commercial organizations donated funds, then the arts could be brought to a wider public.

5 Which sentences are used in exercise 4 to indicate someone else's opinion?

6 Match the statements a–h with the best explanations 1–8.

   Example a 4

   a Amateur arts groups should be given financial support.
   b The wealth of a nation is connected with scientific development.
   c Science is now playing a more important role in our lives than in the past.
   d The work of artists should be censored.
   e Scientists should have some involvement with artists, and vice versa.
   f Science is dull and boring.
   g Many scientific experiments are dangerous to society.
   h The work of scientists should not be tightly regulated by society.

   1 Modern economies cannot advance without a strong scientific base.
   2 Bringing these two groups together would be better for society as a whole.
   3 It has an effect on everything we do from eating to travelling.
   4 Such groups help to develop talent and bring people together.
   5 Certain works of art that are produced are offensive and should be banned.
   6 By limiting scientific work, we might stop certain beneficial developments.
   7 There are many examples where serious mistakes have been made.
   8 Spending time alone in laboratories without much human contact is not very interesting.

7 Read the example and then join your answers in exercise 6 using the phrases in the list below or similar phrases.

   Example
   Some people think that amateur arts groups should be given financial support. *They argue that* such groups help to develop talent and bring people together.

It is argued by some people that	They claim that
Yet others believe that	They feel that
Many people think that	They maintain that
A commonly held belief is that	They argue that
Some people feel that	

Note You can also contradict the opinion: Some people think that amateur arts groups should be given financial support. *However*, I feel that …

Technique

Give opinions of others in order to support your opinion and also to introduce an opinion you want to contradict later.

8 Use the expressions in the box below to develop the explanations in exercise 6.

Example
They argue that such groups help to develop talent and bring people together. *A good example here is* where a young artist joins a local group and progresses on to TV work.

> For example, ▪ For instance, ▪ A case in point is/are … which
> A very good example here is ▪ Take … , for example. It/They

Hypothesizing

1 Match the sentence halves a–e with the endings 1–5.

   a Personally, I would argue that science need not be
   b However, it could possibly be a requirement for the first two or three years,
   c During this time, children can do exciting experiments,
   d If trips to places of scientific interest are also arranged,
   e Above all, I think it is better for science classes to be optional

   1 this might motivate some children to take up a science subject.
   2 obligatory at this level.
   3 because not all pupils are good at such subjects.
   4 like making basic chemical compounds or collecting plants.
   5 as it would give pupils a taster.

2 The sentences in exercise 1 form a paragraph. Why has the writer chosen to use words such as *would*, *could* and *might*? Which sentence asks the reader to imagine a situation and its consequence?

3 The linking devices *if*, *providing*, *provided*, *as long as* and *unless* can all be used to hypothesize. Read the example. Then rewrite sentences a–d using the linking device given.

   Example
   A nation should nurture the talents of its people. It will then reap many benefits.
   If a nation nurtures the talents of its people, it will reap many benefits.

   a Without being encouraged by parents and teachers, aspiring musicians will not develop.
      Unless _____

   b Science may one day stop the ageing process in humans, but will this benefit mankind?
      If _____

   c If there is no effort made to keep traditional farming methods alive, they will disappear.
      Unless _____

   d If innovation is encouraged, many new jobs will be created.
      As long as _____

4 Complete the following sentences using your own ideas.

   a Provided parents have an interest in music, _____
   b If government support for arts projects is not available, _____
   c Unless entrance to museums and art galleries is free, _____
   d Providing young scientists are given the right opportunities, _____

> **Technique**
> Use linking phrases like *if* and *unless* in your answers to Task 2 questions in order to hypothesize about effects.

Practice Test 7

Task 1

You should spend about 20 minutes on this task.

The charts below show how selected age groups bought concert, cinema and theatre tickets online over the first three months of 2013 in three countries and how the Internet was accessed.

Summarize the information by selecting and reporting the main features, and make comparisons where relevant.

Write at least 150 words.

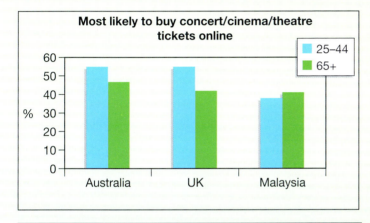

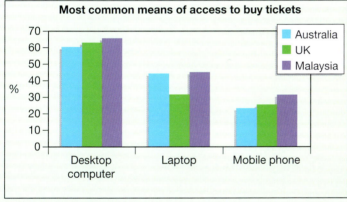

Task 1 Checklist

1 Paraphrase the rubric for both charts.

2 Write an overview for the first chart beginning with an adverb or adverbial phrase like *Clearly* or *It is clear that*.

3 Support the overview by adding specific details to form a paragraph.

4 Do the same for the second chart to form another paragraph.

5 Summarize the two charts in one or two sentences beginning with an adverbial phrase.

Task 2

You should spend about 40 minutes on this task. Write about the following topic:

The money spent on space research has brought enormous benefits to mankind, but it could be more usefully applied. To what extent do you agree or disagree?

Give reasons for your answer and include any relevant examples from your own knowledge or experience.

Write at least 250 words.

8 Nature

UNIT AIMS

| TASK 1 | Making predictions
Ensuring factual accuracy
Making predictions in the past | TASK 2 | Using articles
Writing conclusions |

Task 1 Making predictions

1 Decide which sources of energy in photos a–d will be common in the future. Give reasons.

2 Answer questions a–d.

   a Which source of energy is most common in your home country?

   b What environmental developments do you think will happen in your country in the near future?

   c What other developments are happening in your country which are not happening elsewhere in the world?

   d What will your country be like in 10 years' time/in 25 years' time?

3 Look at the bar chart and description below. Then answer questions a–c.

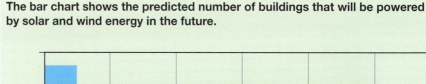

The bar chart shows the predicted number of buildings that will be powered by solar and wind energy in the future.

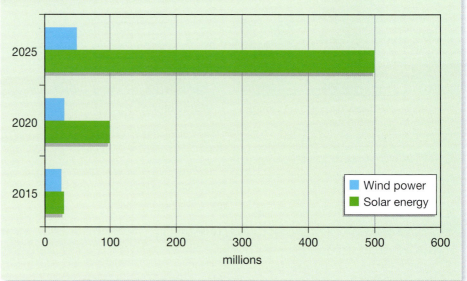

   a What does the chart show?

   b What do the numbers relate to?

   c What is the range of the numbers along the bottom of the chart?

4 Complete sentences a–d with the words *will*, *prediction* or *predicted*.

a The number of solar-powered buildings _____ increase to 500 million in 2025.

b It is _____ that the number of solar-powered buildings _____ increase in the future.

c The _____ is that the number of buildings powered by solar energy _____ increase.

d The number is _____ to increase to 500 million in 2025.

Technique
Use the structure *will* + infinitive or a range of prediction verbs to talk about future statistics. Use the forms: *It is predicted (that)* ...; *... is/are predicted to* ... Before you start writing, make a list of 'predict' verbs to use as trigger words.

5 Answer these questions about the sentences in exercise 4.

a Which of these words could replace the word *prediction*?

> projection ▪ assumption ▪ forecast ▪ anticipation

b Which of these words could replace the word *predicted*?

> projected ▪ anticipated ▪ forecast/forecasted ▪ said

c Which other words could you replace *prediction* and *predicted* with?

6 Complete sentences a–h with the correct forms of the verbs in brackets.

a It _____ (predict) that in 2030, solar energy _____ (provide) energy for 500 million buildings worldwide.

b In 2020, about 25 million buildings _____ (expect) to receive energy from wind power.

c In 2030, much more energy to power buildings _____ (come) from solar energy compared to wind power.

d In the future, solar energy _____ (forecast) to be a much greater source of energy than wind power.

e In the future, wind power _____ (not expect) to be as great a source of power as solar energy.

f In years to come, it _____ (project) that wind power _____ (be) a less important source of energy than solar energy.

g Solar energy _____ (set) to assume greater importance as a source of energy in the future.

h In 2020, it _____ (anticipate) that solar energy and wind power each _____ (provide) approximately the same amount of energy.

7 Which of the sentences below describes something in progress at a time in the future? Which describes something that will happen before a future time?

a By 2025, 500 million buildings *will have converted* to solar power. (*will have +* past participle)

b In/By 2025, 500 million buildings *will be using* solar power. (*will be + -ing* form)

8 Complete sentences a–e with the correct form of the verbs in brackets. Use *will* + infinitive, *will have* + past participle, or *will be* + *-ing* form. You may also need to use the passive.

a In 2025, it is expected that 30 million buildings _____ (use) wind power.

b By 2025, it is predicted that many animals _____ (become) extinct.

c In 2020, more bicycles _____ (sell).

d By 2030, very few people _____ (live) in the countryside.

e By the year 2020, it is anticipated that many natural habitats _____ (destroy).

9 Write at least three sentences about your country or a country you are familiar with. Use these structures: *It is predicted/expected/forecast(ed) that/....... is predicted/expected/ forecast(ed) to ...*

Ensuring factual accuracy

1 Look at the charts. They provide information about reforestation around the world in the future. Answer questions a–d.

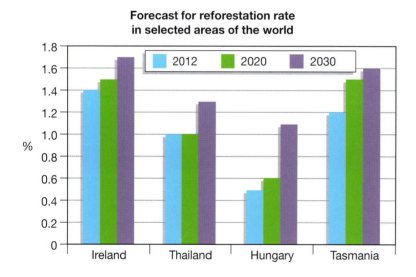

Forecast for reforestation rate in selected areas of the world

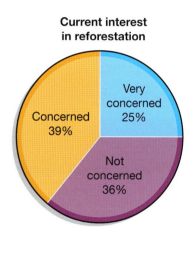

Current interest in reforestation

a In general, is reforestation projected to increase or decrease?
b Which country is predicted to have the highest rate?
c For which country does the chart show the greatest difference between 2012 and 2030?
d In general, are most people concerned about reforestation or not?

2 Find and correct four factual errors in the information below for the task in exercise 1.

> The charts show forecasts for the annual deforestation rate in selected countries.
>
> It projected that Ireland will have the highest rate in 2030 at 1.5 per cent, followed closely by Tasmania. The forecast for both regions for 2020 is the same at 1.5 per cent. It is anticipated that the figure for Hungary will climb from 0.5 per cent in 2012 to 0.6 per cent and then rise more sharply to 1.2 per cent.
>
> From the pie chart, it can be seen that there is some obvious concern about the need for planting more trees ('concerned' 39 per cent, and 'not very concerned' 25 per cent), while at same time there is a sizeable proportion of people who are not concerned.

3 In each of sentences a–f there is a word missing. Add the missing word.

   a It predicted that the use of solar energy will become more important.

   b We see from the chart that largest amount of money was spent on the water conservation project.

   c The chart shows the different types of trees are found in different regions.

   d From the pie chart, can be seen that hydroelectric power constitutes seven per cent of the world energy demand.

   e It is clear that majority of people are very concerned about climate change.

   f Recently, a number of campaigns have encouraged people plant trees.

4 Look again at the text in exercise 2. There are two missing words. Add the missing words in the correct places.

Making predictions in the past

1 Read the table, which describes in thousands the estimated and actual numbers of houses built in the UK by region in 2010. Answer questions a–h to identify the correct facts.

Regions	Estimated	Actual
Scotland	3,200	3,000
Northern Ireland	2,500	5,000
Wales	2,900	6,300
North of England	9,300	13,500
Central England	8,100	16,200
Southern England (exc. London)	51,100	77,500
London	24,800	47,800

   a What information does the table give?

   b How many regions of the UK is it divided into?

   c Usually, was the estimated number above or below the actual number?

   d In which three regions were the highest numbers of houses built? How did the figures for these regions compare with the estimates?

   e Which region had a difference of just over four thousand between the estimate and the actual figure? What were the figures for this region?

   f Which other two regions followed the usual trend? What were the figures for these two regions?

   g In which region was the lowest number of houses built?

   h Which region is an exception to the general trend? What were the figures for this region?

2 Using the facts identified in your answers to exercise 1, summarize the table by selecting and reporting the main features, and make comparisons where relevant. Write at least 150 words.

Technique

Use the structure 'would + infinitive' to talk about predictions in the past. Use the form *It was predicted that … would*. Use contrast link words to compare estimated and actual figures.

Task 2 Using articles

1 Describe the problems that you think will occur in the city shown in the picture.

2 Answer questions a–d.

    a What are the most serious threats that the natural world is facing in the twenty-first century?

    b What is the most serious threat to the environment in your country?

    c What action is being taken?

    d What further steps do you think could be taken?

3 The paragraph below has been taken from an essay on measures to reduce river pollution throughout the world. Complete the gaps with the nouns in the box. The first one has been done for you.

> factories ■ pollutants ■ action ■ fish ■ wildlife
> ~~problem~~ ■ leisure ■ incentives ■ pressure

By far the best way to solve the **1** _____*problem*_____ of water pollution would

be to locate all **2** _____ away from rivers and lakes and to install

waste treatment centres. All the **3** _____ in the water would then

be destroyed, as has been done in many old industrial areas in Poland and

Germany. This would mean that **4** _____ and **5** _____

would be able to return to rivers and people would be able to use them for

6 _____ like swimming and fishing. There is considerable

7 _____ on many poor countries to develop their economies and

so it would be difficult to persuade many of them to change their policies.

However, I think that **8** _____ needs to be taken and perhaps

financial **9** _____ from richer countries would help.

> **Technique**
> Use *would* or the second conditional to talk about a measure and its imagined effects.

4 Are the nouns in the list below countable or uncountable?

> animal ■ information ■ nature ■ climate ■ accommodation
> knowledge ■ research ■ weather ■ tree ■ idea ■ situation ■ fact

5 Look again at the paragraph in exercise 3. Are the answers countable or uncountable?

6 Add *a/an*, *the*, or *no article* to sentences a–h.

    Examples

    The plastic bottles that I threw out yesterday have been taken away for recycling.

    Plastic bottles are now being made of _____ biodegradable materials. *(no article)*

    a _____ knowledge about the environment can be found in _____ books and on the Internet.

    b _____ energy can be generated from biofuels.

    c Trees help to protect _____ soil by conserving water.

    d Newspapers now use _____ high percentage of _____ recycled paper.

    e Looking after _____ nature is important for all of us.

    f It is better to see animals in _____ wild than in captivity.

    g _____ solution to the problem is to fine people for dropping _____ rubbish.

    h _____ new plastic containers which I bought last week are not harmful for the environment as they are biodegradable.

7 In each extract a–f, there is one mistake relating to articles. Correct the mistakes by adding and/or deleting a word.

Example
Animals like chimpanzees and apes should not be used for ~~the~~ experiments.

a Wave power technology is the best answer to the problem of pollution. However, the introduction of such technology also creates the different problem.

b Governments worldwide should tax the cars more. A measure like this would make people think more about nature.

c In near future, houses will be more energy-efficient than they are now.

d Food industry could pay for recycled bottles as was done in the past. The bottles would then not be thrown away.

e Insects like the bees, for example, play a vital role in most ecosystems. The bee pollinates plants and flowers.

f The facilities like dams and forests are also used for leisure.

Writing conclusions

1 Read the two Task 2 questions below. Then decide which question each sentence a–g relates to. Write 1 or 2 next to each sentence.

> **1** *Pollution from aircraft is one of the main factors responsible for global warming. What measures could be taken to reduce this source of climate change?*

> **2** *When a country becomes richer, the natural environment suffers. It is not possible for a country to both develop its economy and protect the environment. To what extent do you agree or disagree?*

a This means that in the short term we will just have to accept paying higher prices for flights and travelling less.

b <u>In conclusion</u>, <u>I do not agree</u> that developing a country's economy has to involve destroying the natural world.

c If this type of eco-friendly business is encouraged, then there is no reason why a healthy economy and a healthy environment cannot exist together.

d <u>All in all</u>, <u>I feel that</u> imposing higher taxes on airlines is unavoidable.

e It is true that some businesses move into new areas with no regard for their effect on the environment.

f We can <u>certainly</u> investigate ways of making aircraft technology cleaner, but we do not know how long they will take to develop.

g However, there are many examples of local businesses which depend on and support the local environment.

> **Technique**
>
> Always write a conclusion to your answer. The conclusion needs to reflect the introduction and summarize the contents of the essay very briefly. It states your opinion, if necessary, or your most important idea, and reminds the reader of how you argued in favour of it.

2 The sentences in exercise 1 on page 67 form concluding paragraphs to the task. Write out the two paragraphs with the sentences in the best order, following the frameworks below.

Question 1

Statement of most important measure:

Another possible measure and why it is less effective:

Restatement of most important measure and its consequences:

Question 2

Statement of opinion:

Reference to the opposite view:

Reason against the opposite view:

Restatement of opinion:

3 Look at the underlined phrases in the sentences in exercise 1 on page 67. For each one, choose two alternatives with a similar meaning from the box below.

> to sum up ■ I believe ■ of course ■ I would argue that ■ in general ■ no doubt
> I do not accept ■ all things considered ■ to conclude ■ I disagree with the idea that

4 Your conclusion must be clear but you need to avoid making claims that sound too strong. One way to avoid this is to talk about possibilities using the phrase *There is no reason why* + negative. Read the example then change sentences a–d in a similar way.

Example
A healthy economy and a healthy environment can exist together.

There is no reason why a healthy economy and a healthy environment *cannot* exist together.

a Local eco-friendly businesses can be successful.

b People could take more holidays at home instead of always flying abroad.

c People could travel by fast train instead of taking short flights.

d Governments should give special financial support to eco-friendly business people.

Practice Test 8

Task 1

You should spend about 20 minutes on this task.

The table below shows the projected costings over the next five years in American dollars for three environmental projects for sustainable forestry. The pie chart shows the expected expenditure breakdown allocation for the first year as the projects are set up.

Summarize the information by selecting and reporting the main features, and make comparisons where relevant.

Write at least 150 words.

	2020	**2021**	**2022**	**2023**	**2024**
West Africa	10.5 million	7.5 million	2.5 million	2.5 million	3.5 million
Central America	20 million	12 million	5 million	5 million	5 million
South-east Asia	30 million	20 million	40 million	50 million	50 million

Projected expenditure in Year 1

- Set-up costs
- Salaries
- Office expenses
- Training

Task 2

You should spend about 40 minutes on this task. Write about the following topic:

More and more city workers are deciding to live in the country and travel into work every day. The result is increased traffic congestion and damage to the environment.

What measures do you think could be taken to encourage people not to travel such long distances into work?

Give reasons for your answer and include any relevant examples from your own knowledge or experience.

Write at least 250 words.

Task 2 Checklist

1. Decide which measures could be put together or developed into a paragraph.
2. Write a short introduction developing the topic.
3. Write two or three paragraphs, giving details about a possible measure in each one.
4. Use trigger phrases like *We could encourage people to travel less by… , People would travel less if… ,* to get some ideas for possible measures.
5. Use trigger words like *for example* to introduce some examples.
6. Write a conclusion summarizing the most important measure and/or why the problem is important.

9 Health

UNIT AIMS

TASK 1 Paraphrasing and using synonyms Checking spelling	**TASK 2** Using general nouns to link and summarize ideas Using cause and effect relationships Ensuring verb-subject agreement

Task 1 Paraphrasing and using synonyms

1 Think of at least one positive and negative effect of each of the developments in health provision in the pictures below. Mention consequences such as cost and relaxed atmosphere.

2 Answer these questions about hospitals and health care.

a What are the main priorities of health care in your country?

b How is health care delivered in your home country? If you want to consult a doctor, what do you do?

c Are medicines free or do you have to pay for them?

d What effect has technology had on medical care in your country?

3 Read the Task 1 question on page 71. Then answer questions a–e below.

a What general statement can you make about the whole graph? Look at the description and the graph itself.

b What general statement can you make about the French hospital?

c What general statement can you make about the Ukrainian hospital?

d How can you link the pie charts to the graph?

e How could you use these words to describe the graph?

> trend ■ upward ■ similar pattern ■ reach a peak ■ except that
> saw a continuous rise ■ change ■ coincide

Task 1

The charts below show the average bed use in three typical hospitals internationally and the proportion of hospital budgets allocated to in-patient care before and after day-surgery was introduced in 2009.

Summarize the information by selecting and reporting the main features, and make comparisons where relevant.

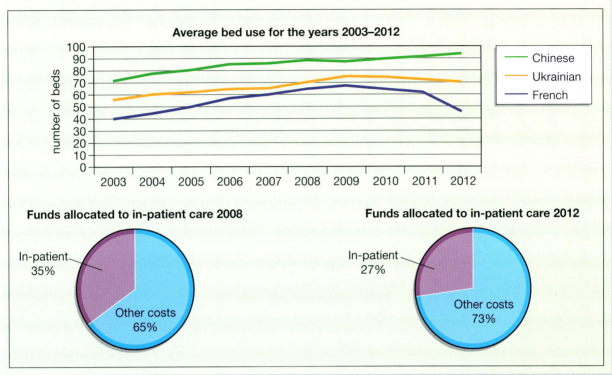

Average bed use for the years 2003–2012

Funds allocated to in-patient care 2008

Funds allocated to in-patient care 2012

4 Complete the text with words from the box. The first gap has been done for you.

> peak ▪ impact ▪ clear ▪ occupancy ▪ trend ▪ ~~details~~
> marked ▪ reduction ▪ falling ▪ significantly ▪ rise ▪ experienced

The graph provides **1** _____*details*_____ about the average beds in use each year in three similar hospitals before and after the introduction of day-care surgery.

Day-care surgery seems to have had an **2** _____ on bed use in all three hospitals. At the French hospital, the figures show an upward **3** _____ over the period from 40 beds in 2003. However, in 2009 bed **4** _____ had reached a **5** _____ of just under 70 beds, before **6** _____ back. A similar pattern was repeated for the Ukrainian hospital, except that the decline in bed use after 2009 was not so **7** _____ (76 beds in 2009 as against 71 in 2012).

The Chinese hospital, by comparison, **8** _____ a continual **9** _____ in bed use between 2003 and 2012, 71 and 93 respectively. However, we see that after 2010 the rate of increase was **10** _____ slower than in previous years.

It is **11** _____ that the fall in bed use coincides with the **12** _____ in the average budget at the three hospitals for in-patient care (35 per cent compared to 27 per cent) between 2008 and 2012.

5 Look again at the words in the gaps in exercise 4 on page 71 and choose a synonym for each one from the box. You will not use all the words.

> effect ▪ use ▪ tendency ▪ cut ▪ considerably ▪ low ▪ evident
> increase ▪ decrease ▪ dropping ▪ information ▪ result
> saw ▪ high point ▪ sharp ▪ dramatically

6 The descriptions below summarize the sentence structure of the text in exercise 4. Number the notes in the correct order, based on the sentences in the text. The first two have been done for you.

a	General introductory statement.	_1_
b	General conclusion based on pie charts.	_8_
c	General statement of first main trend, then specific data.	
d	General statement about a reinforcing trend, then specific data.	
e	Specific statement qualifying the trend, without detail.	
f	General statement about the line graph.	
g	General statement of contrasting trend, then specific data.	
h	Specific statement qualifying the trend, with detail.	

7 For each sentence a–g, there are three alternative phrases to replace the phrase in italics. Delete the option which is NOT correct.

a The graph *provides* details about bed use. (*gives/says/shows*)

b The introduction of day-care surgery *had an impact on* bed use. (*had an effect on/had an affect on/affected*)

c Bed use *reached a peak* of just under 70 beds. (*reached its highest point/reached a height/hit a peak*)

d A similar *pattern* was seen in the Ukrainian hospital. (*design/trend/movement*)

e The Chinese hospital, *by comparison*, continued to see a rise. (*by contrast/on the other hand/alternatively*)

f The number of beds rose from 40 to *around* 45. (*approximately/about/towards*)

g There was a reduction in the budget (35 per cent *compared to* 27 per cent). (*as opposed to/as against/in contrast with*)

h The change in bed use *is reflected in* the budget. (*can be seen in/can be viewed in/can be detected in*)

Technique

Keep a record of synonyms and paraphrases of parts of text. Aim to use these when writing your answer to avoid repetition. Record your synonyms with a context and by theme if possible.

Checking spelling

1 In each group of four words, circle the one which is spelt incorrectly and correct it.

a	therefore	opposite	befor	limit
b	believe	achieve	recieve	brief
c	staying	stayed	studing	studied
d	usefull	helpful	hopefully	carefully
e	personaly	practical	usually	normal
f	efficient	sufficent	ancient	deficient
g	unfortunately	improvement	definitly	management
h	comfortable	diffrent	temperature	interested
i	choise	price	increase	advice
j	preferred	committed	refered	happened

2 Look again at your answers in exercise 1. Some of the spellings depend on simple rules. What spelling rules explain the misspelt words? Compare your ideas with the key on page 110.

3 Find and correct the spelling mistakes in the following sentences. One of the sentences has two spelling mistakes.

a The numbers declined gradualy and stood at just twenty in 2006.

b In-patient care took up 25 per cent of the funds, wich was an increase of six per cent on the previous year.

c A number of significant changes occured in the following twenty years.

d The percentage increased sharply and reached a pick in 2003.

e The figres rose from approximatly 45,000 to 49,000 over the period.

f Patient numbers rose steadily for the first ten years, and then flactuated around 500 for the following decade.

g The required number of beds exeeded what was anticipated for that year.

h Most people in the servey thought that more money should be spent on the health service.

4 Read the following extract written by an IELTS student on the number of traffic accident victims seen at a local hospital. Find the eight mistakes that he made.

> The averag number of road traffic acidents from cars increased dramaticaly between 1995 and the year 2000, rising from a total of 53 to 178 respectively. Over the next five years, there was a noticeable improvment as numbers fell steadilly to a new low point of 37 in 2006. As regard motorcycl accidents, however, it is clear the trend is upward, with more occuring in this category in the later period.

Technique

Make a note of words that you have spelt wrongly in the past. In each word, underline the part that you tend to get wrong or write/ highlight this part in another colour.

Task 2 Using general nouns to link and summarize ideas

1 Decide which of the items below are the most important for good health. Add at least one other lifestyle factor to the list.

> taking regular exercise ■ carefully monitoring your diet ■ having a wide range of interests
> having a wide network of friends ■ living in the countryside ■ sleeping at least seven hours a night

2 Complete the paragraph by choosing the best adverb in each case.

> The **1** *normally/outlandishly/strangely* beneficial effect that animals have on people's health and general well-being is now **2** *essentially/goodly/well* recognized. The idea may seem peculiar to some people, but **3** *surprisingly/shockingly/unpredictably* there is clear evidence of the partnership. Take the example of dolphins, which are **4** *wildly/widely/hardly* known for their healing qualities. Dogs have also been used to detect cancer cells very **5** *deeply/professionally/accurately* in patients and are **6** *often/rarely/hardly* even taken around hospital wards to be introduced to **7** *seriously/hugely/deadly* ill patients. The effects of this particular partnership are **8** *importantly/really/well* documented and have led to animals being used **9** *frequently/seldom/lots* to supplement conventional medicine.
> **10** *Evidently/Clearly/Oddly*, the message is that more money should be used to research how animals can benefit humans.

3 Which list of general nouns summarizes the paragraph in exercise 2?
  a situation – examples – effects
  b situation – effects – reasons – examples

4 Complete sentences a–i with a general noun from the box.

> idea ■ information ■ issue ■ knowledge ■ measure ■ opinion ■ problem ■ scheme ■ solution

  a The best way to improve public health is to provide people with all the facts, but the
  _____ needs to be made simple.

  b It is often suggested that national health systems should be modernized. However, many
  people are opposed to the _____ of modernization.

  c Our programme to introduce new equipment succeeded in reducing waiting lists, but the
  improvement _____ met with considerable resistance.

  d The government should invest more money in preventing drug abuse. This _____ ,
  if taken, would save many lives.

  e Obesity is on the rise in many countries and not just in the developed world. It is now an
  _____ that demands immediate attention.

  f More nurses need to be trained rather than doctors. This, I feel, is the best _____
  to the current crisis.

  g People are often aware of the dangers of smoking, but even with this widespread
  _____, it is difficult to persuade them to stop.

  h Some people are against the involvement of private companies in health care, but this
  _____ is held by fewer people nowadays.

  i Lack of health care is making the lives of many people miserable, yet it is a _____
  that can be easily tackled.

5 For each of a–h, read the first sentence. Then complete the follow-up sentence with your own ideas. Use the general noun in italics to help you.

a Some people are concerned that increasing numbers of old people will mean more spending on health care.

This *issue* _____

b Conventional and alternative medicine can complement each other.

This *idea* could _____

c In the future, health care will be much cheaper for everyone.

This *prediction* _____

d The level of change within many national health systems is increasing.

Initially, this may be a *problem*, but _____

e Health care costs are now worrying planners throughout the world.

The *situation*, however, _____

f More emphasis should be put on preventive medicine, like health education.

Measures like this _____

g Acupuncture is becoming more and more popular around the world.

Not surprisingly, it is a *trend* _____

h If people live longer, this can lead to other costs and problems.

This is a *matter* that _____

> **Technique**
>
> Use *the/this* + general nouns to help you link sentences. This is an alternative to using linking devices such as *moreover*, etc and adds variety to your writing.

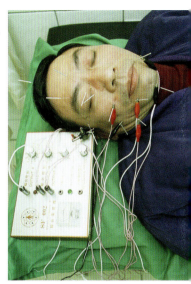

Using cause and effect relationships

1 Choose one of the topics a–c below. Make a list of ideas for the topic you have chosen. Use the general nouns in the box to organize and trigger ideas.

a the connection between music and health
b how alternative therapies can influence health
c the connection between exercise and health

> conclusion ■ effect ■ idea ■ information ■ issue
> knowledge ■ matter ■ measure ■ opinion ■ prediction
> problem ■ scheme ■ solution ■ trend ■ view ■ example

2 Make a short plan for your idea using a cause and effect chain:

| the connection between music and health |
| ↓ |
| music improves health |
| ↓ |
| it can help people relax |
| ↓ |
| relaxation makes people happy |
| ↓ |
| happiness improves health |

> **Technique**
>
> Keep a list of cause and effect verbs and collocations: *make, produce, result in, cause, affect, improve, have an effect/have an impact on, lead to*.

3 Write a paragraph based on your ideas in exercise 1. Remember to give reasons and examples, using the plan in exercise 2.

Unit 9

Ensuring verb-subject agreement

1 Complete the following sentences with *is*, *are*, *has* or *have*.

a The number of people who are suffering from stress _____ on the increase.

b The fact that people live longer nowadays _____ led to an increased number of elderly people in society.

c Predictions about how long a patient with cancer will live _____ often inaccurate.

d A ban on advertising all types of junk food _____ probably the only way to stop the spread of obesity.

e The pressurized situation in many hospitals _____ resulted in a stressed workforce and low morale amongst nurses.

f Elderly people who have a large family _____ generally healthier and happier than those who have fewer contacts with other people.

g The reason why allergies are becoming more common _____ still not known.

h An increasing number of patients seem to be dissatisfied with conventional medicine and _____ turned to alternative therapies.

Technique

Check that the subjects and the verbs in your sentences agree. Remember that the subject is not always the closest noun to the verb, e.g. *the number of people rises each year* (not *rise* because the verb agrees with *number*, not people).

2 In sentences a–g, replace the countable nouns in italics with an uncountable noun from the box. Make any other necessary changes in verb forms or pronouns.

> progress ■ evidence ■ information ■ work ■ advice
> research ■ equipment

Technique

Remember many general or collective nouns like *information* are uncountable in English. Make a list of common uncountable nouns like these, with examples of their use.

a Everyone is aware today of the bad effects of smoking on people's health. These *facts* are published all around us, even on cigarette packets.

_____

b Most doctors recommend a diet low in sugar and fat, and high in fibre. Unfortunately, these *suggestions* are not often followed.

_____

c Many nurses nowadays do not carry out basic care such as washing and feeding patients. Instead, these *tasks* are carried out by health care assistants.

_____

d Enormous *advances* have been made in understanding how disease spreads, but the possibility of a worldwide pandemic is still with us.

_____

e Many people enjoy keeping fit in the gym by using rowing machines, walking machines, and so on. However, these *devices* can be dangerous if they are not used properly.

_____

f Many doctors do not believe in homeopathic medicine. However, there are certainly some *indications* that it can be beneficial.

_____

g Some *studies* have been carried out which show that elderly people live longer if they live with a partner.

_____

Practice Test 9

Task 1

You should spend about 20 minutes on this task.

The graph below shows the average monthly use of a health club in Miami, Florida by all full-time members in 2013. The pie charts show the age profile of male and female members.

Summarize the information by selecting and reporting the main features, and make comparisons where relevant.

Write at least 150 words.

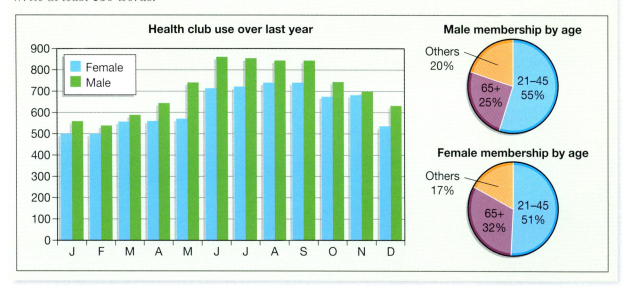

Useful language

men/women who used the health club …

male/female health club users …

members aged between 21 and 45 …

members aged 65 or over …

other age groups …

In general, the health club was used more …

The number of users rose/increased/decreased/declined gradually in January/from January to March/between January and March

21 to 45 year olds made up/accounted for …

Task 2

You should spend about 40 minutes on this task. Write about the following topic:

The number of elderly people in the world is increasing. What do you think are the positive and negative effects of this trend?

Give reasons for your answer and include any relevant examples from your own knowledge or experience.

Write at least 250 words.

Useful language

As far as the workplace/home life/the economy is concerned …

One obvious disadvantage is …

Another drawback …

One benefit associated with …

Societies with a greater number of older people …

If a country has a substantial number of elderly people …

Elderly people are more/less likely to …

UNIT AIMS

TASK 1 Using the correct word order
Linking information and data
using *with*
Task 1 revision

TASK 2 Using the appropriate paragraph
structure
Distinguishing between relevant
and irrelevant information
Task 2 revision

a

b

Task 1 Using the correct word order

1 Describe the role of money in the lives of the people in photos a and b.

2 The list below contains factors which influence career choice. Choose the three that have influenced you most in choosing a career then answer questions a–e.

> money ■ interest ■ friends ■ ambition ■ role models ■ parents ■ teachers

a Why have you chosen these three factors?
b How did they contribute to your career choice?
c Why did you not choose the other factors?
d What other factors might influence you?
e Which factor has influenced your choice the most?

3 Read the Task 1 question. Then answer questions a–e.

Task 1

The bar chart shows the results of a Greek survey from two selected age groups in 2012 on the relative importance of five factors in choosing a career.

Summarize the information by selecting and reporting the main features, and make comparisons where relevant.

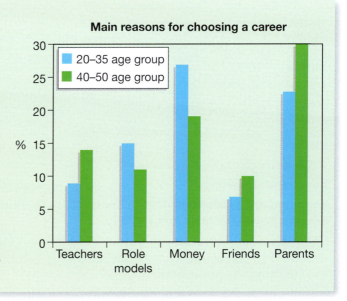

Main reasons for choosing a career

- 20–35 age group
- 40–50 age group

%

Teachers | Role models | Money | Friends | Parents

a What does the chart refer to?
b What do the items along the bottom of the bar chart refer to?
c What are the most noticeable features of the younger age group?
d What are the most noticeable features of the older age group?
e What differences can you see in how the factors were rated by the younger and older age group?

4 Reorder the words in italics in the text below describing the chart in exercise 3 on page 78.

The bar chart provides information from a Greek survey about **1** *reasons the/for/main/career/a/choosing* among two age groups, 20–35 and 40–50.

It is clear that the two groups **2** *the/influenced/were/various by/factors* to different degrees, with the most influential factors which contributed to career choice for the 20–25 age group being money (approximately 27 per cent) and then parents (23 per cent). However, the factors **3** *the/age/were/for/reverse/group/the/40–50*, with parents affecting them most at 30 per cent. **4** *teachers/as/regards/role/and models*, the relative importance of each was again the other way round: **5** *nine/fifteen/and/respectively/group/per/cent/for/younger/the*, and 14 and 11 per cent for the older.

6 *similarity/only/the/the/two/groups between/age* was that friends had less influence over career choice for the younger and older groups **7** *factors/than/any/other*, seven and ten per cent respectively.

5 Six of the eight sentences a–h contain a word in the wrong place. Correct the sentences by moving the word to the right place.

Example
Traveller numbers have decreased over period in the question.
Traveller numbers have decreased over *the* period in question.

a The specialist sales of tours have fallen recently.

b In 2010, more males than females took up individual sports rather than team activities.

c As can be seen, more people from the younger age group travel on their own, in sharp contrast to those over sixty.

d It is clear that the number of flats by single people in occupied major cities in the West is putting pressure on housing.

e From the graphs, it can be concluded that are young people much more mobile than previous generations.

f The noticeable pursuit of a professional career among both men and women has led to a reduction in the birth rate.

g There are similarities in the presentation of the several data.

h Overall, the chart shows that the media people are responsible for turning into celebrities.

Unit 10

Linking information and data using *with*

1 Read the example sentence from the text in exercise 4 on page 79. Then answer the questions below.

Example

However, the factors were the reverse for the 40–50 age group, with parents affecting them most at 30%.

- **a** What function does the phrase beginning with *with* introduce?
- **b** What type of verb structure normally follows *with*?

2 Read the example. Then join the sentences below making any necessary changes.

Example

There were several similarities. The most and least important factors were the same.

There were several similarities, *with* the most and least important factors being the same.

- **a** Sales were upward for most of the year. Profit reached a peak in December.

  _____

- **b** The main reason for career choice was ambition. 50 per cent chose it.

  _____

- **c** It is expected that the price of one-bedroom flats will rise. Accommodation for individuals is in short supply.

  _____

- **d** The pattern was different. Passenger numbers dropped in summer and rose in winter.

  _____

- **e** The trend was clearly upward. Manufacturing costs decreased at the same time.

  _____

- **f** Consumption of energy rose. The highest point was in January.

  _____

Task 1 revision

1 Decide if the following statements about Task 1 techniques are true or false.

- **a** Your first paragraph is usually a general statement about the subject of the graph, table, map, etc.   True/False
- **b** Writing in paragraphs is not important for Task 1.   True/False
- **c** Task 1 will always be written in the past tense.   True/False
- **d** If your English is correct, then it does not matter if your information is inaccurate.   True/False
- **e** You need to decide which is the most important or striking information in the graph, table, map, etc.   True/False
- **f** You should quote all the figures that the information gives you.   True/False
- **g** In a paragraph, sentences which quote specific figures nearly always come before general statements.   True/False
- **h** Your overview will not normally give specific figures.   True/False

Task 2 Using the appropriate paragraph structure

1 For each Task 2 question below, put the sentences that follow in the most logical order to create a paragraph.

> **1** *Ambition is a negative attribute of a person's character. Do you agree or disagree with this statement?*

a This is because, even when they realize an ambition, they are still not satisfied.

b It is certainly true that ambitious people do not always create happiness for themselves or others.

c If we look at the businessman who wants to earn a six-figure salary, we see that in most cases, when he reaches this position, he will still want more power or an even higher salary.

> **2** *Particular cultures are under threat nowadays due to the fact that we are living in a global village. What do you think can be done to protect a society's traditional values and culture?*

a Nor does it mean that they will fail to respect and value other people's cultures.

b One way to protect traditional values and customs is simply to teach people to value their own culture.

c On the contrary, it will give them the confidence to operate in our global village without feeling that their own identity is under threat.

d This does not mean that they have to resist the current movement towards greater international trade.

> **3** *Emails are the most valuable tool for communication in the twenty-first century. To what extent do you agree or disagree?*

a They can exchange ideas and discuss things more often as they are working, and the result may be a better end product.

b This allows people to work together on the same project even if they are on opposite sides of the world.

c Emails have certainly had far-reaching effects on people's ability to communicate.

d It is now possible for people to correspond cheaply and at length from anywhere as long as they have a connection.

2 Match each of the paragraphs you made in 1–3 in Exercise 1 with the correct structure below a–c.

a general statement – reason why this statement is true – example

b general statement – reason why this statement is true – effect – second effect

c statement of what should happen – statement that a negative result will not occur – statement that a second negative result will not occur – positive result

3 Read the following two Task 2 questions. For each one, choose one of the paragraph structures in exercise 2 on page 81 and write a paragraph which could form part of an answer, following the structure you have chosen.

> *Money does not make happiness. To what extent do you agree or disagree?*

> *It is better to reform criminals instead of just punishing them. What measures could be taken to attempt to integrate law-breakers back into society?*

Distinguishing between relevant and irrelevant information

1 The three paragraphs below relate to the Task 2 questions in exercise 1 on page 81. In each paragraph, there are several options. Choose the options which are most relevant to the question.

Text 1

1 Another reason why ambition is not always good is that ambitious people may use unfair or dishonest means of reaching their goal. For example, they may
  a work so hard that they neglect their families.
  b take the credit for work that they have not done.
2 In some cases, they may damage the careers of people who they see as competition, perhaps by
  a telling lies about them to their employers.
  b stealing their money and possessions.
3 In the most extreme cases, they may turn to serious crime. _____ provides a clear example of this.
  a Shakespeare's story of Macbeth
  b The story of Sinbad the sailor

Text 2

4 One way to ensure that people value their traditional culture is to focus on language. With the global dominance of English, some minority languages such as _____ may feel under threat.
  a Welsh or Estonian
  b Chinese or Arabic
5 If people are made familiar with the history and literature of their own language, then
  a they will be more able to talk to older people about it.
  b they will appreciate their own culture more.
6 This could be done by arranging arts festivals or writing competitions.
  For example, in the UK
  a there are many prizes which novelists and poets can win.
  b there is an annual festival to celebrate the best of Welsh writing and culture.

Text 3

7 However, the effects of the Internet on communication are not all positive.
  Emails can be written and replied to very quickly which means that
  a people often do not consider carefully what they have written.
  b people can check their inbox two or three times a day.
8 Another problem is that people simply send and receive too many emails. _____
  The result of this is that they spend time dealing with this constant stream of messages instead of doing their real work.
  a Children, for example, love to contact their friends frequently by email.
  b An office worker, for example, may receive more than thirty emails a day.

2 Read the Task 2 question. Then answer questions a–c below.

Task 2

The current interest in famous people's private lives has negative effects both for those people and for society as a whole. Newspapers should not be allowed to publish details of people's private lives unless it is clearly in the public interest.

To what extent do you agree or disagree?

a   Think of a famous person who has been in the news recently for something unconnected with his/her job. What were the effects of this?
b   How relevant is your example to the question? If possible, compare your example with a partner. Which is the most relevant to the question?
c   Write a general statement–example paragraph, using the example you have chosen.

Task 2 revision

1 Read the Task 2 techniques in the questionnaire. Decide how often you do these things.

Tick the appropriate box.	Always	Sometimes	Never
I match the organization of my essay to the question.	☐	☐	☐
I use the paragraph structure.	☐	☐	☐
I divide my essay into paragraphs.	☐	☐	☐
I use general nouns to help develop my sentences and paragraphs.	☐	☐	☐
I use a range of linking devices – *because, for example* – to trigger my ideas.	☐	☐	☐
I write a short introduction which paraphrases the question.	☐	☐	☐
I know that I must write at least 250 words.	☐	☐	☐
I leave myself time to check my answer.	☐	☐	☐
I develop functions like *advantages, disadvantages, solutions, measures, causes* by using *reasons, examples, results, effects*.	☐	☐	☐
I can state my opinion clearly and contradict other opinions.	☐	☐	☐

2 Which phrases can you use as trigger words for each of the following functions? Make your own lists.

a   Example: *For example,* _____
b   Reason: *because* _____
c   Effect: *As a result,* _____
d   Additional information: *Moreover,* _____
e   Hypothesis: *If* _____
f   Contrast: *but* _____
g   Concession: *Although* _____
h   Conclusion: *And so* _____

3 Some functions are related so that one suggests the other. Complete the list below with related functions. Are the combinations fixed or can you combine them in any way?

   a Problem and _____

   b Measures and _____

   c Cause and _____

   d Reason and _____

   e Example and _____

   f Effect and _____

   g Additional information and _____

   h Condition/Hypothesis and _____

   i Concession and _____

4 Read the Task 2 question below, then use the trigger words to develop sentences a–f with your own ideas.

Task 2

Too much emphasis is put on earning money rather than looking for a good quality of life. To what extent do you agree with this idea?

   a Money is not as important as friends, because _____

     _____

   b For many people, keeping fit and healthy is the main factor which is necessary for a good quality of life. However, _____

     _____

   c If one is content with life, then _____

     _____

   d What is involved in achieving a good quality of life depends on many factors rather than just one. For example, _____

     _____

   e Happiness and contentment are more important than the pursuit of freedom. The latter aim

     _____

   f Many people living in poor housing conditions are still happy. So the idea that _____

     _____

5 Write your own paragraph about the importance of family in maintaining a good quality of life. Write about 60–80 words.

Practice Test 10

Task 1

You should spend about 20 minutes on this task.

The line graph below shows the number of people in Great Britain living alone by age from 1996 to 2012.

Summarize the information by selecting and reporting the main features, and make comparisons where relevant.

Write at least 150 words.

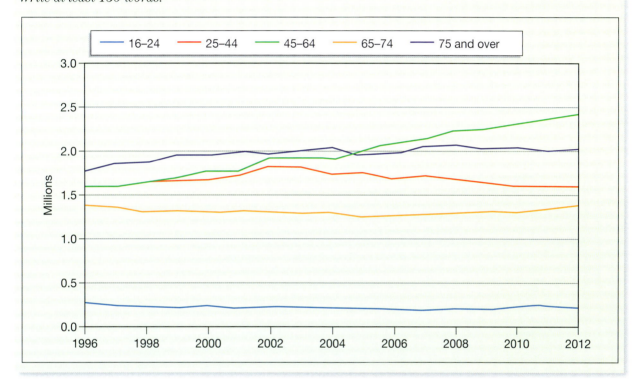

Task 2

You should spend about 40 minutes on this task. Write about the following topic:

Individuals can do nothing to change society. Any new developments can only be brought about by governments and large institutions. To what extent do you agree or disagree?

Give reasons for your answer and include any relevant examples from your own knowledge or experience.

Write at least 250 words.

Model
and sample answers

This section contains both model and sample answers. The model answers provide examples of good answers. The sample answers are written by students with possible score bands. The publishers stress that these are not official grades and are for guidance only. There is no guarantee that these answers would obtain these grades in the test.

Practice Test 1

Task 1

The graph shows the percentages of homes in the UK which had access to four items of modern technology between 1994/95 and 2008. For all of these four items, the percentage showed a clear upward trend.

In 1994/5, about 48 per cent of homes had a CD player. This figure rose gradually over time to reach around 90 per cent in 2004. There was little change in the percentage after that. The number of households with mobile phones stood at just under 20 per cent in 1996. This also increased over the period and reached approximately 80 per cent in 2004/5. After that, this figure also levelled off.

Turning to houses with Internet connections, the percentage rose from around 10 per cent in 1998 to just over 60 per cent in 2008. No figures are given for households with DVD players before 2002/3. The percentage rose steeply from around 30 per cent at that time to about 80 per cent in 2004/5. It then continued to increase, but more gradually. *(162 words)*

Comments: Paragraph one paraphrases the topic and gives an overview of the general trends. Paragraph two gives details for CD players and mobile phones, as these two items showed similar trends. It quotes the percentages for the beginning of the period and the highest points. Paragraph three gives details of the remaining two items.

Task 2

Most people face important changes at some point in their lives. These new situations can be exciting, but they can also be difficult for people to cope with.

One reason for this difficulty is that new situations bring new challenges. People will have to do things that they have not done before or learn about subjects that they have not thought about before. They may therefore feel that they are not capable of dealing with the new situation.

Another reason is that many changes often come at the same time. For example, if someone moves to a new part of the country, they do not just have to get used to the place. They also have to form new friendships and probably start a new job. With all these new changes coming together, it is easy to feel overwhelmed by it all.

One key to dealing with change is information. People tend to be frightened of the unknown, so they should always find out as much as possible about the new situation before making the change. Another measure is simply to be patient and not expect everything to work out perfectly at the beginning. For example, if someone starts a new job, they will probably experience difficulties with some aspects of it at first but, with time, they will gain the knowledge and experience they need.

In conclusion, it is important for us to be prepared for changes in our lives both by being well informed about the kinds of new situations we may find ourselves in and by giving ourselves time to adapt to them. *(266 words)*

Comments: Paragraph one introduces the topic. Paragraphs two and three give reasons why people find it difficult to adapt to new situations. The second reason is developed with an example. Paragraph four then gives two measures, and again the second one is developed with an example. Paragraph five concludes by referring to the importance of the topic and summarizing both measures.

Practice Test 2

Task 1

The graph shows the contribution of different sectors to the UK economy in the 20th century. In particular it compares the agricultural, manufacturing and business and financial sectors.

Firstly, agriculture sector shows the higher value at the beginning of the period (around 50% in the first 50 years of the century). By the 1975, it had suffered a dramatic decrease (15%) followed by a drop to almost zero in 2000. By contrast, business and finantial sector were almost zero at the beginning but it sharply increased during the period.

Manufacturing sector seems to follow the trend of agriculture, starting with a value of 45% in 1900. In 1950 it began to fall till 1975 where it was below 35%. At the end of the period the percentage for manufacturing reaches 20%.

In general, agricultural and manufacturing sector has a similar trends but the former dropped much more at the end of the century than the latter. In contrast, the trend of business and financial increased during the period. *(168 words)*

Grade: 6

Comments: Use of the rubric unchanged reduces the word count. The information is logically ordered, but the business sector data is omitted. Vocabulary is adequate and usually appropriate, as is the range of sentence forms, but there are some significant errors.

Task 2

Studying the past certainly plays an important, if not the most important role in helping young people deal with today's world.

There can be no doubt that studying history can help young people to operate in the present world. For example, studying the history of their own country not only gives them pride in their own history and culture, but an understanding of why the business, financial or legal systems work as they do. They can then learn to judge what to protect and what to change. Learning history can also help prevent people from making mistakes by showing them how events develop and mistakes occur, thus enabling them to avoid pitfalls in their lives.

Although studying history is beneficial, it is not enough on its own. There are other approaches that are almost as important in helping young people. Travelling informs the young about the world around them. Take educational exchanges between countries like Russia and the UK, for example. In such exchanges, learning about the culture and history, the ways of doing things as well as learning the language take place. These, in turn, help young people deal with people from other countries as well.

Another measure is to make sure that all young people are equipped for the digital age. They need a wide range of digital skills to study and find work in a highly competitive world. Even with these skills, an understanding that comes from a study of culture and history both national and international is still needed, to survive and not make the mistakes of the past.

In conclusion, while there are obviously different ways to help people deal with modern life, an awareness of the past is probably the best means of doing so. *(292 words)*

Comments: The model answers each part of the question. The writer answers the first question (To what extent do you agree or disagree?) in the second paragraph. The third and fourth paragraphs answer the second question (What other measures could be effective in helping young people to function well in the modern world?). The answer is divided into suitable paragraphs: an introduction, three body paragraphs and a conclusion.

Practice Test 3

Task 1

The diagram illustrates the various stages in the desalination of seawater to make it suitable for drinking.

First of all, water is taken from the sea and then passed through a pre-treatment filter where the big impurities are removed. This backwash is then piped back into the sea through another filter. At the next stage in the process, the remaining water is forced through a membrane at high pressure and any impurities including salt are removed. After that, the seawater concentrate is returned to the sea while the remaining water goes through a post-treatment process. In this phase, the water is treated with lime, chlorine and fluoride to make it drinkable before it is stored in a reservoir. Finally, the desalinated water is distributed to the integrated water supply system for people to use as drinking water.

Desalination involves a process of purification of water followed by filtration and adding chemical agents. *(153 words)*

Grade: 7

Comments: Interest is maintained by the flexible use of input language, and a wide range of vocabulary and skilfully deployed grammatical structures. All stages are covered accurately, though some additions are made. The overview would work better as the second sentence.

Task 2

Great changes have taken place in our life along with development of society. As far as I am concerned, the Internet plays a big part in this.

First of all, with the opportunity of surfing internet or playing computer and video games, people have a more sedentary life style. Children no longer play games outside and get exercise but they spend time on the computer. This has bad effect on their health and can cause problems such as obesity.

Another problem is the negative effect on their relationship with their family. Internet access fills most young people's time, and even their leisure time, so this is the cause of their disconnection with their family and ultimately can have an effect on their social behaviour. A third problem is that not all internet sites are useful. Information is often not accurate and some sites are not suitable for children. Some internet sites like chat rooms can even be dangerous because you do not know who is the other person.

As regarding children's use of the Internet, the first solution must be with the parents.

They need to limit hours that children spend on the computer and to encourage them to have other hobbies and pastimes. There is an important need for them to spend more time to speak with their family than an electronic connection. Parents should also encourage children to use other means of information in addition to internet.

To conclude, I would say that the internet has brought many benefits and it will not disappear, therefore it is very important that we learnt to use it well so that we can reap the benefits and not the disadvantages. *(278 words)*

Grade: 7

Comments: The topic is considered fully, with ideas presented in a clear progression with mostly logical paragraphing. A good range of vocabulary gives flexibility and precision to the writing. Sentence structure is reasonably varied, but minor grammatical errors are frequent.

Practice Test 4

Task 1

The chart provides information about the proportions of males and females in the UK by age group in 2009 who did not have any qualifications.

Among those aged 17–19 and 20–24, more males than females lacked qualifications, approximately 7% and 6%, and 8% and 7% respectively. As regards the 25–29 age group, there is no difference in the proportions of men and women without qualifications at around 8% for both sexes with the same pattern being seen for the 30–39 age group. By contrast, among those aged 40–49, the lack of qualifications was greater among women compared to men (12% as opposed to 10%), while more women in the oldest age group (about 20%) did not have any qualifications compared to around 17% for men.

Generally speaking, it is clear that there is a greater proportion of men compared to women without qualifications in the youngest age groups whereas the reverse is true for the oldest age groups. *(159 words)*

Comments: This is a good model answer. The introduction is a paraphrase of the rubric and there is a clear overview at the end of the answer. The answer is divided into paragraphs. All the data is compared and there is a range of vocabulary and grammatical structures, including complex sentences.

Task 2

To some extent I disagree with the notion that competitive sports cannot be part of the school curriculum. However, the amount of time given should not be overlooked.

Sports as a whole is an important part of growing up. Students regardless of their age take part in exercise individually or as a team member. Take primary schools for instance, they have playgrounds and fairly enough facilities from which students can take benefit.

In secondary schools students' attitude to sport changes. The demand for more facilities and equipments rises. As can be seen, more and more teenagers turn to football, swimming, even body building outside school hours. They try to make use of the facilities available to them at school as well. What is important is time which should not be spent on taken up sport and not doing other school work or study.

On the other hand, considering the availability of the facilities to all schools is not a bad idea.

To illustrate this, some schools are well equipped while others do poorly. No matter how little the facility students should be encouraged to take part in competitive sports.

All in all, I think sport was part of everyday life in the past and is in today's sport attracting societies. The best place you start your life after home is school. Everyone decides what to do at early age. As for sport, it was part of curriculum vitae in the past and will be in the future of course, with a better time management. *(254 words)*

Grade: 6

Comments: Though the ideas are relevant and sufficient, faults in ordering and use of links sometimes cause difficulty for the reader. A good range of vocabulary is mostly used with precision. A limited but accurate range of complex sentences are deployed.

Practice Test 5

Task 1

The maps show how the seaside town of Templeton changed between 2000 and 2013. Overall, it is clear that the town underwent a considerable transformation over the period.

On the west side of the river, a number of developments occurred. Blocks of flats replaced the houses north and east of the lake with more houses also being built to the south. Between the sea and the extension of the railway along the sea front, the houses and trees gave way to more blocks of flats and a supermarket.

On the east side, a new airport was constructed northwest of the school with new houses being put up north of the hospital. The railway in the east of the town was extended south and then along the sea front. A car ferry was built in the southeast with a factory replacing the houses and the trees.

The town appears to be more built-up and less green in 2013 compared to 2000. *(159 words)*

Comments: This is a good model answer, which covers all the key points. There is a clear overview in the introduction with a further comment at the end. The answer contains a range of vocabulary and the sentences are well constructed with a variety of structures.

Task 2

Many people thinks that the world existing problems are only matter the young generation as they are the candidate who are facing them now and in the future.

Although a considerable percentage of the public might refer to these hazards as hazards for the young predominantly, yet many of these concerns are actually brought into the scene by the old people. The previous generation are those who lived the new developments in science and technology that brought with them pollution, poverty and part of it also possible distinction of many species of plants and animals.

So they raise the alarms for those radical and serious consequences. It is often suggested that old generation are passing by and not interested in what happening and only the young who gives those alerts considerable thoughts.

However from what we are expecting now that many of green people are old and work actively to reserve animals rights and fight fiercely against global warming and environmental pollution. This give us that the present world concerns are a shared interest of both old and new generations. Although many activist on these issues appears in the media and they are from the youth, still and probably equal number from the old follow the same routes.

Actually no one in this life want to destroy our planet. Definitely every parent is of concern about his offspring lives thereafter, and selfishness does not dominate our thinking at all. What one should be aware of is that such threats are not always discussed or contemplated in the right way by old or young generation. *(264 words)*

Grade: 6

Comments: Though the ideas are relevant and sufficient, faults in ordering and use of links sometimes cause difficulty for the reader. A good range of vocabulary is mostly used with precision. A limited but accurate range of complex sentences are deployed.

Practice Test 6

Task 1

The table illustrates the percentages of both young boys and girls who listened to music in the previous month in the capital of Japan.

The most striking feature is that males were more interested in music than their female counterparts except for listening to CDs (19% and 22% respectively). The highest rate was 79% for boys who were interested in MP3 players, while with regard to the same type of players for girls the proportion was 40% which was almost similar to the percentage of the Internet (42%). With respect to live music, females recorded 44%.

Turning to the pie chart, 70% of young Japanese people prefer live music, whereas recorded music rate was 26% and those who answered Don't know their rate was just 4%.

In conclusion, young females spent less time listening to favourite music compared to the opposite sex. Regarding preference of music Live music scored the top percentage. *(150 words)*

Grade: 6

Comments: The key points are mainly covered, but there is an important error (paragraph 3). It could be ordered more logically. However, cohesive devices are well used. Vocabulary is adequate for the purpose. There is a variety of sentence structures, but their complexity sometimes causes difficulty for the reader.

Task 2

It is often said that nowadays we are living in a global village. People make contact with those from other cultures far more than fifty years ago, both during leisure and as part of their work.

The obvious advantage of this is that it contributes to international understanding. If, for example, British people learn something of other languages and learn to relate to others regardless of their race, then there will be less tension between people from different backgrounds from other countries even within Europe.

There are clear advantages for businesses as well. If business people are culturally aware, they may be able to adapt their products such as food books to suit new customers abroad and enter new markets. They can also draw on a wider pool of talent when looking for staff if they are not limited to recruiting people from their own culture. These new members of staff may bring new ideas and approaches to the workplace.

The main disadvantage probably occurs when the contact with the other culture is only brief. A short superficial experience of another culture can give people mistaken ideas about it, because they may make generalisations about what they have experienced which are not true. By contrast, reaching a good understanding of another culture takes time and requires people to remain open-minded.

In conclusion, contact with people from other cultures is of benefit both for people's personal development and for a country's economy. However, we should be aware that building up a good awareness of another culture can be a long process and should not just be based on one or two limited experiences. *(272 words)*

Comments: Paragraph one introduces the topic. Paragraphs two and three give two main advantages for being in contact with people from different cultures. Paragraph four describes a situation when it may not be beneficial. Paragraph five concludes by referring back to both advantages and to the situation when it may be a disadvantage.

Practice Test 7

Task 1

The two bar chart illustrate the percentage of purchase on-line tickets of concert, cinema and theatre in (Australia, the UK and Malaysia), by a selected age group and how the interest was accessed over the first three months of 2013.

Purchases for the age group 25–44 was the same in the western countries at 55%, whereas in Malaysia, it was just under 40%. Surprisingly, the percentage was very close in the UK and Malaysia around 40% for the age group 65+, with a slight increase in Australia to about 45%.

In terms of the most common means of access to buy tickets, the chart shows that the desktop computers was the predominant means in Malaysia the UK and Australia at about 60%, 62% and 68% respectively. Next came the laptop, with a close percentage in Australia and Malaysia around (45% each), while there was a moderate drop to 30.5% in the UK.

The data might give us an indication about the online purchasing. *(163 words)*

Grade: 5

Comments: Excessive use of the rubric reduces the word count and incurs a penalty. There are many inaccuracies in the data, which lacks an overview. Vocabulary and links are inaccurately used, but grammar and sentence structures are adequate for the task.

Task 2

The question of whether money could be more usefully applied to tackle the crisis around the world rather than spent it on space research is a very controversial issue and it is now a matter of considerable public concern. There are, therefore, people on both sides of the argument who have feelings either for or against.

Many people believe that money should be spent to solve food crisis in Africa and South Asia. Drought, for example, left Africa with famine. Every 30 seconds an African child dies of hunger and about 45% of children in South Asia suffer from malnutrition. Similarly, the global issue is the conflict of AIDS in Africa. Although, there are numerous factors in the spread of HIV/AIDS , it is largely recognized as a disease of poverty. Medicines, for instance, are very expensive and the government in poor countries can not afford to treat the disease, therefore millions are dying, while in rich countries people are living longer.

Having said that, however, some people oppose the former argument. They claim that space research has brought enormous benefits to mankind. Recently, NASA has launched Satellites for weather and climate, which will give the scientists a unique view of earth's atmosphere, helping them to improve their abilities to forecast weather and predict climate change.

From what has been discussed above we may draw the conclusion that both points of view have their merits. Although, human life has priority in our societies, advanced research should be carried out to find another source of energy, water on other planet, and to understand the planets and its' effect on earth for the benefit of all. *(276 words)*

Grade: 7

Comments: Though there are sufficient ideas and evidence, the first paragraph adds nothing. Ideas are logically organized and paragraphed, but the conclusion is not clearly articulated. There is a good range of vocabulary and sentence structures, despite some jarring punctuation errors.

Practice Test 8

Task 1

The table shows the estimated costs of environmental projects in three different areas. The pie chart gives a breakdown of the costs in the first year.

In 2020, the projected cost for the West African project is 10.5 million dollars. It is forecast that this figure will fall to just 2.5 million in 2022 and 2023, but it is expected it will rise to 3.5 million in 2024. The Central American project is predicted to cost 20 million in the first year but by 2022 annual expenditure will have fallen to 5 million. It will then remain unchanged. However, in South-east Asia the projected cost for 2020 is 30 million and expenditure will reach 50 million in 2023 and 2024.

According to the pie chart, 50 per cent of the budget for year one will be spent on salaries and 30 per cent on set-up costs. Training and office expenses will each make up 10 per cent of the total. It is clear that by far the greatest amount of money will be spent on the South-east Asian project and, unlike the other two, annual costs will rise. *(183 words)*

Comments: Paragraph one paraphrases the rubric. Paragraph two gives details about all the projects and gives an overview by pointing out the differences between the third project and the previous two. Paragraph three gives details about the pie chart.

Task 2

Many people are moving out of big cities into the countryside to live to escape from city problems. This is causing problems because most the jobs that are available are in the cities so people have to travel back into the cities again to work. The transport system cannot cope so people are using their own cars and the countryside is affected by the traffic jams.

One solution to encourage people to stay in cities is to improve the quality of life there. More money could be spent reducing crime, as this is one of the main reasons why people leave cities. For example, more policemen can be employed for city centres, which happened in New York and is happening here in UK. As well as safe places to work and live city centres could be made more friendly and welcoming. The environment can be made cleaners and more agreeable to live and work in. This way people might be encouraged to stay rather than moving out.

A very different way to tackle the problem would to move some of the jobs out of city to smaller cities or towns. People could then still live in the countryside and enjoy it and only have to travel short distances to work. Another step is to encourage workers to spend part of their working week at home, perhaps two days and then to go into work in the other days. This is happening more and more in many parts of the world.

There are other ways to overcome the situation but these are the most important. *(264 words)*

Grade: 7

Comments: The writer's proposals are clearly presented, with logical paragraphing, but the conclusion could be more fully developed. The progression of ideas is well marked. The vocabulary is very appropriate to the task. Sentence structures are reasonably varied, without significant errors.

Practice Test 9

Task 1

The graph gives information about the average monthly use of a Health Club in Miami Florida by full time members in 2013.

One of the most striking features of the graph is that use the gym was higher in summer compared to the other months of the year. In January 550 males visited the gym the figure decreased slightly. After that there was a significant increase in the number of males membership from January to June. In June the figure hit the highest point of 8500 but in July there was a slight reduction to December. The trend for females membership follow the same. However from July to September 7200 females used the gym in every month.

Turning to pie chart, 4% more of male membership aged between 21 and 45 used the facilities in gym compared to females. Thirty-two per cent of female member had age 65+ in contrast to 25% of males. Twenty per cent of other age group among males had the membership compared to 17% of females.

Overall, higher number of males used the gym than women. *(179 words)*

Grade: 5

Comments: Copying the rubric reduces the word count. Data is listed mechanically and includes serious errors. The selection, which is not wholly logical, lacks an overview. The range of both vocabulary and sentence structures is limited, with many grammatical errors.

Task 2

There is no doubt that age expectancy has increased over the last twenty years. The question of whether the increasing number of elderly people causes positive effects or negative is a matter of dispute. As far as I am concerned it has negative effect for a number of reasons.

Some people are of the opinion that this trend should be increased because there might be more experienced workers in society. People will work longer than now. This might have a possitive effect on economy. As we know, these people give tax to the government.

Moreover if we ask anyone, they are happy to live longer as they devote most of their lives to working. In retirement age elderly people need comfort and such people desire to do many things that they did not do before. Thus, increasing aged population gives hope to the seniors who would like to enjoy their lives.

However, I do believe that higher aged population needs higher investment as people in elder age suffer from diseases such as heart disease, stroke, diabetis, Alzehamer disease.

Governments need to invest a colosal sums of money treating such patients. Further more people in elder age become more dependent to others as these people nee to be supervised by other people. I think nobody likes to live with other people and use the facilities that are not belong to them. Therefore seniors suffer from depression and psychological problems.

At the same time if people work longer, there is not promotion for the younger generation because most positions are occupied by the elderly people.

To conclude, I feel that the negative effects on society outweigh the positive effects because of the above reasons. *(282 words)*

Grade: 6

Comments: There are plenty of ideas, but the paragraphing is not well managed. However, the sentences tend to be clearly linked. The range of vocabulary is adequate for the purpose, as is the variety of sentence structures, but grammatical errors are obtrusive.

Practice Test 10

Task 1

The line graph shows the number of people in the UK living on their own between 1996 and 2012. It is clear that for most age groups there was relatively little change over the period.

The group who were least likely to live alone were the 16-24 year olds. About one quarter of a million lived alone in 1996 and the figure remained largely unchanged. Among 25 to 44 year olds, about 1.6 million lived alone in 1996. There was a slight rise in the number between 2000 and 2004 but it had dropped again by 2012.

For the oldest age groups, those aged between 65 and 74 and those aged 75 or over, there was again little change. For the first group, the figure stood at around 1.4 million and for the second there was just a slight rise from about 1.8 to 2 million.

There was, however, a more significant change among 45 to 64 year olds. In this case, the figure was about 1.6 million in 1996, but rose to reach nearly 2.5 million in 2012. *(187 words)*

Comments: Paragraph one paraphrases the rubric and gives an overview. Paragraph two gives details about the youngest two groups. Paragraph three gives details about the oldest two groups. Paragraph four gives details about the remaining group and points out that this group shows a different trend.

Task 2

There is little doubt that governments and large institutions implement many innovations into our society. However, from my point of view, they are only able to do so with the help of ideas from individual citizens.

For a start, every part of society, including government and large institutions, consists of individual members. Governments have the rights to the further use of the new ideas and in fact should always listen to them. For example, a Ukrainian engineer called Platon introduced the idea of building a bridge across the river in Kiev. Seeing the strategic importance of this bridge the government provided funds to build it. And now the whole of society benefits from the use of one man's idea.

Furthermore in London, the Mayor, Mr Livingstone, announced a competition which can be entered by individuals to find a new way to provide air conditioning for the underground system. This is yet another example of how governments and large institutions rely on the creativity of individuals to be inventive and bring about change.

Some people might say that governments have the strength, power and money to realize and introduce new ideas on their own. In the case of institutions they possess up to date equipment and massive facilities. However I would say that they are not enough to allow them to contribute to society as a whole. This is where creativity and outstanding ideas come in. So if an individual's efforts are combined with the governments' s power and money, there would be many changes that could benefit everyone.

In conclusion, both individuals and large organizations, including governments need to work in partnership to bring about any beneficial change. *(278 words)*

Grade: 8

Comments: The writer does not fully address the topic but does present a clear and logically sequenced argument, supported by evidence. Cohesive devices are used effectively. The range of vocabulary produces fluency and precision. Sentence structure is varied and grammatically accurate.

Key

Unit 1

Task 1

Describing trends

1
1 iPod/MP3 player
2 tablet
3 plasma TV
4 games console

2
Possible answers:
RISE: increase, soar, go up, shoot up, surge, rocket, jump, leap, climb, improve
FALL: decrease, drop, come down, go down, plummet, tumble, slump, decline, dwindle

3
Possible answers
The graph associated with iPods may be expected to be increasing gradually [c], the tablet graph may be expected to be increasing slowly then sharply [f], the graph associated with plasma TVs may be expected to be fluctuating but rising upwards [d] and the graph for games consoles could be decreasing before levelling off [h].

4
2 c	3 d	4 a
5 b	6 h	7 f
8 e	9 h	10 e

5
2 rose
3 fluctuated
4 fluctuated
5 dropped
6 fell, levelled off
7 rose, climbed
8 declined
9 decreased, levelled off
10 dropped

6
Slow: steadily, gradually, slightly
Fast: wildly, sharply, dramatically, suddenly

Using nouns to summarize

1
fall, rise, increase, decline, drop, fluctuation, improvement, reduction, growth

2
a There were wild fluctuations in spice exports from Africa over the period.
b There was a gradual fall in the development of new products.
c Research investment has decreased noticeably.
d There was a significant drop in the purchases of tickets last month.
e There was a dramatic rise in the number of sites on the Internet.
f The sale of mangos decreased suddenly.
g The number of visitors at the theme park fluctuated very slightly.
h Sugar imports declined gradually.
i There has been a slow increase in the quality of food in supermarkets.
j There was a remarkable fluctuation in the number of air travellers.

3
a African spice exports
b product development
d ticket purchases
e Internet sites
f mango sales
g theme park visitors
i (supermarket) food quality
j air traveller numbers

Understanding data

1
a $160,000	b $85,000
c $125,000	d $120,000
e $130,000	f December
g January	

2
a months of the year
b thousands of dollars
c Sales went up for Internet Express, Wi-fi Café, and Café Cool, but down for The Tea Room.
d Between different cafés and between different months for the same café.

3
2 noun	3 verb	4 noun	
5 adverb	6 verb	7 verb	

4
1 d	2 g	3 e	4 f
5 a	6 c	7 b	

5
a As regards   b By contrast
c Furthermore, Likewise

Task 2

Understanding questions

1
a drawbacks   b reasons
c causes   d solutions

2
b disadvantages, agree or disagree
c advantages/benefits, disadvantages
d agree or disagree
e agree or disagree, measures
f causes, solutions/measures
g views

3
b three parts, two statements plus question
c two parts, statement plus question
d two parts, statement plus question
e three parts, statement plus two questions
f three parts, statement plus two questions
g two parts, statement plus question

Two statements are often given to contrast both sides of the argument; two questions are often given to ensure that both the advantages and disadvantages are discussed or to discuss the problem then offer solutions.

Expressing solutions

1
Possible answers
Housework takes much less time than it used to; people can be contacted anywhere and can use their phones to use the Internet and keep up with emails; journey times from place to place and country to country are much faster.

2

Possible answers

Work: people have less stable jobs

Technology: new computer systems and electronic devices are continually being developed

Travel: air travel is still on the increase and becoming cheaper

Communication: people are using text messages, email and online messaging more frequently

Health: life expectancy is increasing

3

Possible answers

Technology is changing continually and the changes are more rapid than in the past.
All kinds of travel are increasing as air and train fares become cheaper. Communication is changing faster than all the other areas.
People's health is improving, but changes in life expectancy are happening less rapidly than other areas of health.

4

a part 1
b causes, solutions
c reasons and examples

5

They are answering: Can you suggest some possible solutions?

They suggest: encouraging workers to relax, providing gyms and massage therapy, training employees to manage their time better.

Results: people will be more efficient and productive; the workplace will be happier.

6

1 c 2 f 3 d 4 a 5 b 6 e

7

a People should be encouraged to exercise more.
b The number of working hours should be reduced.
c One possibility is for the government to provide each employee with their own computer.
d Parents could be persuaded to spend more time with their children.
e The number of cars coming into cities should/could be restricted.
f If the government built more skyscrapers, the problem should/could be solved.

8

a obesity (or stress)
b stress
c lack of technology
d lack of discipline
e traffic congestion
f overcrowding

9

Possible answers

b As a result, people would be obliged to manage their time more effectively.
c This would enable them to work from home and avoid stressful commuting.
d This would lead to better communication between members of the family.
e Consequently, there would be less traffic congestion and journey times would be reduced.
f By doing this, they would ensure that there were fewer people living in crowded or substandard accommodation.

Using linking devices

1

addition: and, furthermore
condition: if
example: for instance, for example
purpose: in order to
reason: because, since
result: consequently, and so, therefore, as a result

Using trigger words

1

Reason: because
Result: As a result, and so
Example: For example
Solution: The obvious answer is

2

Possible answers

A

If people migrate to cities, they become trapped in poor, overcrowded accommodation and so their health deteriorates. As a result, their quality of life may be no better than before. A good idea would be to try to create new jobs in the countryside. By doing this, people would not feel the need to move into cities which are already overcrowded.

B

People spend too much time watching TV. For example, some children stay up late watching TV in their bedroom instead of getting a good night's sleep. Consequently, they arrive at school tired and unable to learn. If households just have one TV in the main living area, then it will be easier to control how many hours are spent in front of it. This could lead to better results at school.

C

The development of tourism often creates negative feeling among local people because tourists do not help the local economy. For example, they may stay in international hotels which make large profits outside the country. The obvious answer is to encourage tourists to use locally available accommodation. Furthermore, by doing this, they would learn more about the country they are visiting.

Unit 2

Task 1

Comparing information

1

a paper money, around eighth century AD
b ballpoint pen, patented 1938 (other dates are Fahrenheit's thermometer 1714, Durand's tin can 1810, and Hunt's safety pin 1849)
c Students' own answers.
d There are many other important historical inventions. They could include paper, the light bulb, the radio, TV, the internet, the tablet.
e Students' own answers.

2

a The bicycle was ranked as the most important invention by most males and females.
b More females than males ranked the bicycle, mobile phone and radio as the most important invention.
c More males than females ranked the car, tablet, Internet and TV as the most important discoveries.
d Students' own answers.

3

a than	b popular
c less	d The least popular
e More	f The most popular
g Fewer	h less important
i than	j less

4

b The bicycle was the most popular invention.
c The car was more popular among males than females.
d The TV was less popular among both sexes.
e Fewer men than women voted for the mobile phone.
f More people picked the bicycle than the other inventions.
g More females than males picked the radio.
h The tablet was more popular for men than women.
i The most popular invention was the bicycle.
j The TV was the least popular invention.

5

Possible answers
Not as many females as males chose the car.
Not as many males as females chose the mobile phone.

6

a More males than females chose the car.
b More women than men selected the mobile phone.
c The Internet was chosen by more males than females.
d More females than males picked the radio.
e Fewer males than females picked the radio.
f The tablet was chosen by fewer females than males.
g The bicycle was selected by fewer males than females.

Using adverbs in comparisons

1

a Slightly	b considerably
c Many	d Substantially
e significantly	f practically
g far	h much
i Nearly	

2

a nearly, practically
b considerably, many, substantially, significantly, far, much
c slightly

3

Possible answers
a Far more males than females chose the car.
b Considerably more women than men selected the mobile phone.
c The Internet was chosen by significantly more males than females.
d Substantially more females than males picked the radio.
e Significantly fewer males than females picked the radio.
f The tablet was chosen by slightly fewer females than males.
g The bicycle was selected by slightly fewer males than females.

Comparing and contrasting

1

Students' own answers.

2

Aerobics, archaeology and painting/art.

3

Possible answers
a The bar chart provides information about the number of people in two different age groups who have various interests.
b Numbers of people.
c Clubs/societies.
d Age groups.
e There is no time reference.

4

Students' own answers.

5

1 c   2 e   3 a   4 f   5 d   6 b

6

Endings that could come first:
2,3,4,5,6
Noun phrase only: in comparison with, compared

7

1 However, By contrast
2 but, while
3 but, whereas
4 far, considerably
5 but, although
6 significantly, noticeably

Task 2

Using it/they/this/these

1

Archaeologists, for example, help us to learn about the past. *They* look for evidence in artefacts like pots and jewellery. *These* reveal a lot of information about our ancestors. *This* is very useful, but *it* is still quite limited.

2

1 d   2 b   3 a   4 c

3

b Old buildings help <u>create a more relaxing environment</u> in cities than concrete office blocks.
c Studying history may <u>trigger an interest in other subject areas</u>.
d Built-up areas can be made more attractive by adding <u>monuments and statues</u>.
e Governments should <u>provide more money to preserve historical sites</u>.
f <u>Tradition</u> does not hold us back as some people believe.
g Schools and colleges need to emphasize <u>history and related subjects</u> …
h <u>The Internet and computers</u> can be used to preserve the past.

4

a it/this	b they
c This	d it, it/this
e it	f it
g this	

5

Possible answers
1 This is often where people do most of their reading now.
2 They are not read in the same kind of depth as books.
3 These are convenient because they contain a great deal of text in a small space, but many people still prefer the experience of holding an actual book.

Planning essays

1

Students' own answers.
Other important historical events could be the discovery that the Earth goes round the Sun, the landing on the Moon, or the first splitting of the atom.

2

Relevant points: b, d, e, g

3

Possible answers

… such as in Ancient Greece or during the Roman Empire.

As a result, they will be able to compare these societies with our own.

Therefore, they will become more aware of the kind of society that we live in.

Furthermore, they will come to appreciate the contribution that these societies made to the way we think today.

4

Students' own answers.

Developing ideas

1

Possible answers

They could visit historical places such as castles or archaeological sites.

They could research their own family history.

They could do project work on historical periods or figures who interest them.

2

	1	2	3
Solutions	a	b	h
Examples	i	e	d
Effects	f	c	g

3

a solution   b effect
c example   d solution
e example   f example
g effect   h solution
i effect

4

Possible answers

One way is to encourage children to study history by using the Internet. For example, they could search for information about historical figures online. This could increase their motivation to do historical research. The best way is probably to visit historical sites. For instance, children could visit a local archaeological site. As a result, the historical places will come to seem more real. Another method is to involve children in doing writing projects, such as producing a poster or an information booklet. The skills that they practise in these sorts of projects could then be applied in other subjects.

Unit 3

Task 1

Using the passive

1

Possible answers

a ring: diamonds, metal
  house: cement, bricks, wood, glass
  laptop: plastic, metal
  shoe: leather, plastic
  car: metal, plastic, glass, rubber
b natural: diamonds, rubber, wood, leather, metal
  manufactured: cement, glass, plastic, bricks

2

1 is extracted	2 is heated
3 is cooled	4 reaches
5 cools	6 condenses

3

1 hold	2 rains
3 fill	4 becomes
5 occur	6 rises
7 begins	8 falls

4

a intransitive
b transitive
c both

Sentence a cannot be put into the passive.

5

Transitive: design, produce, send, manufacture, obtain
Intransitive: rise, die, become
Both: begin, dry, grow, cool

6

Possible answers

a After the motorcycle is designed, a prototype is made. It is tested and the motorcycle is manufactured. After this, it is exported and sold.
b First the wheat is planted, and later the crop is harvested. The wheat is transported to the mill where it is made into flour. The flour is bought by a baker. Later the bread is baked and sold.

7

1 b   2 c   3 a   4 h   5 d   6 e   7 f   8 g

8

Active: died and dropped, lived, turned, built up
Passive: was formed, was covered, was trapped, is now mined

Sequencing

1

a from the coal mine by delivery lorry
b by conveyor belt
c oxygen
d raw syngas
e carbon dioxide, mercury and sulfur
f purified syngas
g It drives/powers it.
h It drives/powers it.
i the turbine
j They are sent to a heat recovery steam generator.

2

Adding oxygen/The addition of oxygen

Removing carbon dioxide, mercury and sulfur/The removal of carbon dioxide, mercury and sulfur

Producing slag/The production of slag

Converting steam into electricity/The conversion of steam into electricity

Generating electricity/The generation of electricity

3

1 First of all
2 After that
3 where
4 From this
5 Following that
6 in turn
7 then
8 subsequently

4

Adverbs: First of all, at first, after that, as a result, consequently, subsequently, otherwise, afterwards, then, furthermore, therefore, in turn
Conjunctions: When, once, where

5

a When the snow falls, it covers the ground with a protective layer.
b As soon as her cubs are born, the lioness licks them all over.
c Once the paper is collected, it is sent for recycling.
d Before volcanoes erupt, they send huge amounts of smoke into the air.
e When the plants transpire, the air becomes humid.
f The trees are cut down and the forest is gradually destroyed.

6

Possible answers

a As soon as the food is processed, it is packaged and then it is distributed.

b When the cycle is completed, it repeats itself all over again.

c After the rubbish is collected, it is sent to a centre for sorting and then it is recycled.

d Once a new model of the bicycle is developed, it is tested.

e When the TV is assembled, it is sent to the shops.

f As soon as the water is purified, it is bottled.

g The data about the weather is collected, and the information is then broadcast.

h Once the prototype has been tested, it is modified.

7

Students' own answers.

Task 2

Using *which* to organize and add information

1

Possible answers

a Computers, automatic doors, mobile phone apps, digital cameras, tablets and satellite navigation systems (GPS) can all help. All of them can also make life difficult as it can take some time to learn how to use them and they can go wrong.

b Automatic doors and TV remote controls might make people lazier. Video games and tablets might also make people lazy because it's simpler to use these instead of taking up more active pastimes.

c Students' own answers.

2

causes, solutions

3

a practical skills for everyday life

b over-reliance on machines

c office functions, opening and locking doors, switching machines on and off

d Workers cannot do basic practical tasks.

e They have difficulty in processing basic information.

f A non-defining clause. The clause in the first sentence is a defining clause.

4

a allow the TV to do their thinking for them at home

b traditional practical skills

5

a Sometimes, computers make mistakes, which wastes valuable time and can cost money.

b TV programmes provide people with information about the world, which is often very useful.

c Machines now give us more freedom, which means we have more time for leisure activities.

d Technology saves us more and more time, which can be used to create more machines.

e More and more household tasks are now carried out by robots, which will be even more common in the future.

f Everything seems to be available at the touch of a button, which makes people expect instant responses from other people.

6

a computers make mistakes

b information about the world

c machines now give us more freedom

d time

e robots

f everything seems to be available at the touch of a button

The *which* clause expresses an effect in a, c, d and f.

7

a The situation, which has now become much more complex, is effectively out of control.

b The problem, which the public blame the government for, is everyone's responsibility.

c The cause of the problem, which is not immediately obvious to everyone, is a lack of basic training.

d The solution which, in my opinion, is by far the best, is to have a day at work where people do not use computers or other machines.

e Office technology, which requires only basic training to use, is the cause of much frustration at work.

8

Students' own answers.

Expressing result and purpose

1

Students' own answers.

2

Paragraph 2

Example: parents no longer have enough time to spend with their children.

Cause: many are working unsociable hours

Effect: young people are deprived of valuable time to learn everday practical skills.

Paragraph 3

Cause: the drive towards learning new technology

Result 1: young people leave school literate in computer skills.

Result 2: a generation deficient in practical skills

Reason: practical skills are squeezed out of the curriculum

Example: carpentry

3

Paragraph 1

Problem: First of all

Cause: A number of reasons have been put forward for this, but by far the most important … is

Paragraph 2

Example: for example

Cause: because

Effect: consequently

Paragraph 3

Cause: also needs to carry a good part of the blame

Result 1: This has led to

Result 2: it has also created

Reason: because

Example: like

4

Result

so

therefore

consequently

as a result

and so

for this reason

as a consequence

hence

which leads to

which means that

Purpose

in order to

so as to

with the aim of

so that

5

Possible answers

a Children are now learning how to do mental arithmetic again, which means that they will rely less on calculators.

b Some cities charge motorists to take their cars into the centre in order to encourage people to use public transport.

c Machines are manufactured to break down after a certain time so that companies can sell more of them.

Unit 4

Task 1

Using general and specific statements

1

Students' own answers.

2

Students' own answers.

3

a The pie charts describe the proportions of each group reading particular numbers of articles each week.

b The numbers represent percentages of people.

c It shows the number of articles read each week. There are three separate categories.

d For all students, the most noticeable feature is that the majority read 1–5 articles.
For PhD students, the most noticeable feature is that the majority read 12 or more articles per week.
For junior lecturers, the most noticeable feature is that the majority read 6–11 articles per week.

e In general, most students read between one and five articles a week.
Most PhD students read more articles than other students and junior lecturers.
A tiny minority of junior lecturers read only 1–5 articles per week.

f In the introduction.

4

a how, and

b For example

c respectively

d whereas

e Meanwhile,

f but, which

g that

5

Possible answers

illustrate = show

weekly = every week

compared to = in comparison with

the overwhelming majority = the vast majority

furthermore = moreover

the pattern = the trend

the corresponding figure = the same figure

it is clear that = it is evident that

6

Paragraph 1: a

Paragraph 2: b, c, d

Paragraph 3: e, f

Paragraph 4: g

7

General: a, e, g

Specific: b, c, d, f

8

General: b, d, e, f, g

Specific: a, c, h

9

1 There are clear differences in the pattern of student enrolment at university in different years.

2 Less than one third of children in rural areas obtained a place at university.

3 Greater numbers of boys choose to study physics than girls.

4 International students make up 21 per cent of the total number of students at university.

5 There is a clear relationship between parental income and children's achievement in school exams.

Paraphrasing

1

a Far fewer junior lecturers read over 12 articles a week compared with PhD students.

b The average junior lecturer reads more journal articles than the average student.

c The average PhD student reads more articles than the other students at the university.

d Those students who are researching for a PhD have more time to read articles than junior lecturers.

Describing proportions

1

a three-quarters

b half

c a quarter

d a third

2

26 per cent, about one in four, just over a quarter;

33 per cent, one third, one in three;

48 per cent, almost half, nearly half, just under one half, close to one half;

75 per cent, three out of four, three quarters

3

very big: vast, overwhelming

very big (used before numbers): massive, hefty

very small: tiny

not very big (used before numbers): modest, mere

4

Possible answers

a about one in four/just under a quarter of

b the overwhelming/vast majority of; 75 per cent

c about one in three/just over one third; one in ten/one tenth

d Fifty per cent; a hefty 64 per cent/over six out of ten

e The overwhelming/vast majority/About nine out of ten

5

a The percentage who spent 8–14 hours in the library are similar: 35 per cent for all students and 32 per cent for postgraduate. The proportions are approximately the same, but for different categories of hours.

b The percentages of students spending 1–7 hours and 15 or more hours are very different in each case.

c As students progress towards postgraduate level, the number of hours spent in the library increases.

d Undergraduate students spend less time than other students in the library. Other students spend less time in the library than postgraduate students. Postgraduate students spend more time in the library than all other students.

6

a pattern   b proportion
c majority   d minority
e trend   f two-thirds
g quarter

7

Students' own answers.

Task 2

Avoiding overgeneralization

1

a They are connected by the topic of education.
b No, they stand alone. The statements are very sweeping and do not clearly support the first one.
c You could give reasons like: *because this would help poorer countries and poorer parts of rich countries develop.* Then you could give examples, like: *For example, schools in places like .... could be sponsored by richer countries.*

2

Both reasons support the opinion.

3

Students' own answers.

4

Possible answers

You may feel that some of the statements are too broad. For example, 'the present generation knows more than the previous one' is obviously not true for everyone in the present generation. It may not be true for all subjects.

5

Possible answers

a It is important that universities should make more links with businesses.
b There is no doubt that the present young generation knows more than their previous counterparts.
c One cannot deny that teaching thinking at school is essential, even at primary level.

d It is impossible to argue against the fact that more time needs to be devoted to learning music, either during or after school hours.

6

Possible answers

e Some people believe physical education is a necessary part of the learning process for all pupils.
f Some people feel that play is a major part of the learning process for children.
g Other people are of the opinion that it is important for children to try to learn another language early in their education.
h Yet other people put forward the view that being bored and learning to deal with boredom is a necessary part of the learning process for children.

7

e 1   d 2   c 3   b 4   g 5   a 6
f 7   h 8

Developing reasons

1

a 3   b 2   c 1

2

Possible answers

a For example, they can learn languages like Japanese or Russian.
b A good example is the endless tests given to schoolchildren in some countries.
c Take, for example, trips to places of historical interest like The Great Wall of China or Istanbul.
d It can, for example, provide small classes and sometimes even better facilities.
e Famous sports stars like footballers could, for instance, conduct training on a regular basis.

3

Possible answers

a Some people are of the opinion that foreign language learning should be compulsory, because it helps intellectual development. It can, for instance, develop one's own language and improve communication.

b There is no doubt that students need to have good study skills on entering university, since most subjects require a lot of sophisticated skills like listening to lectures and note taking.
c Yet others feel that university lecturers need some teacher training, as they are used to lecturing rather than teaching which is not suitable for small groups. Lecturers could, for instance, follow short courses or visit colleges or schools.
d It is important that boys and girls be educated in separate schools. One reason for this is that they learn in different ways. For example, boys are known to prefer competitive activities.
e Some people think that teachers' salaries need to be as high as doctors' or lawyers' since they have such an important job to do. For instance, creating a future generation of doctors and lawyers requires good well-paid teachers in the present.

Unit 5

Task 1

Describing changes

1

a Sandra
b Tom
c Dave

2

Possible answers

a Dave thinks it was worse. There is now more for young people to do. Sandra thinks it was better. It was quiet and peaceful. Now there is a bypass. Tom agrees the town was prettier and more peaceful. However, he thinks there are more jobs and opportunities.
b Students' own answers.
c Dave: The ice rink, the leisure centre, and the skate park were opened by the council last year. Sandra: A bypass and an industrial estate were built a few years ago.
d Students' own answers.

3

a The town changed considerably over the period.

b It was less residential.

c There were fewer trees in 2010.

d They were dramatic.

e The construction of the stadium and the removal of the houses.

f The houses were torn down and the trees were cut down. This was done to make way for skyscrapers.

4

2 residential

3 experienced

4 noticeable

5 houses

6 factories

7 facilities

8 construction

9 corner

10 comparison

5

1 It tells you that the maps show how Youngsville has developed.

2 The second sentence.

3 South of the river west of the railway.

4 North of the river.

5 West to east.

6 rural, urban

6

a The town centre was developed dramatically.

b The neighbourhood was completely transformed.

c The residential area was totally reconstructed.

d The old factories were totally redeveloped.

e The old houses were rebuilt.

f The entertainment district was completely modernized.

7

a The town centre developed dramatically.

8

a The map shows changes which *took place* between 1990 and 2010.

b Very few trees *remained*.

c Over the next 25 years, all these houses were *knocked down*.

d The houses *made way* for skyscrapers.

e The trees *were cut down*.

f The area *experienced* dramatic changes.

g The woodland *made way* for a golf course.

h A marina *was also built*.

9

a was knocked down

b was cut down

c was redeveloped

d was converted

e underwent

f was pulled down; replaced

g was constructed

h took place

i was transformed

10

d 'Over the past seven years' cannot replace *Between 2005 and 2012*.

11

a By 2012, the row of old houses had been knocked down to make way for a road.

b By 2012, the forest had been cut down to build a railway.

c By 2012, the area had been redeveloped completely.

d By 2012, the factory had been converted into an art gallery.

e By 2012, the city centre had undergone a total transformation.

f By 2012, the row of old terraced houses in the city had been pulled down and replaced by a block of flats.

g By 2012, a sports complex had been constructed in the suburbs.

h By 2012, a number of spectacular changes had taken place.

i By 2012, the whole centre of the town had been transformed by new developments.

Describing locations

1

a It is south west of the stadium.

b It is to the south of the golf course.

c It is north of the skyscrapers.

d It is in the south-west of the town.

e It is south of the river.

f It is in the north-east of the town.

g It is just to the north of the river mouth.

2

a in	b by	c beside
d in	e from	f on
g beside	h on	i off

3

Students' own answers.

Task 2

Developing and justifying opinions

1

Students' own answers.

2

a You can agree 50 per cent or disagree 50 per cent. You have to express an opinion.

b Young employees should receive the same amount of money as older people if they do identical work.

3

b Contradiction	c Example
d Explanation	e Reason
f Reason	g Result

4

a Many people believe that

b However

c Take, for example,

d They deserve to receive the same salary …

e because

f Moreover,

g which

5

Students' own answers.

6

Delete the following:

1 Moreover	2 while
3 And	4 also
5 however	6 Subsequently

7

1 a contrast	2 b reason
3 a addition	4 c example
5 a result	6 c conclusion

8

Possible answers

a Many feel that young people today have much more influence in the world than past generations. Personally, I believe that this is not necessarily true, because most people in power belong to the older generation. For example, most politicians throughout the world are mainly middle-aged. Moreover, most wealth is concentrated among people in their forties upwards. So, young people may appear to exert influence, but it is limited.

b According to some people, older workers are just as equipped to deal with the modern world as young people. However, I think that younger people are much more prepared because they are much more computer-literate than older people. Moreover, they are well-acquainted with the latest 'gadgets'. For example, many young people are able to design their own web pages and adapt quickly to the latest tools. Thus, I feel they are better at coping with today's world.

c Some people feel that modern advertising encourages a negative view of older people and older workers. This is because companies often choose to show young people using their products. Nevertheless, I feel that this may be changing. A number of recent advertisements have shown older people in positive roles both in the family and the workplace. As the average age of the country's population increases, advertisements like this are likely to become more common.

Writing introductions

1
a 1   b 4   c 2

2
Possible answers
Some people feel that blogs are just a waste of time and another way to lure people on to the Internet. Personally, however, I feel that they are very useful for people of all ages, especially young people, for many reasons.

Unit 6

Task 1

Writing overviews

1
Students' own answers.

2
Students' own answers.

3
Students' own answers.

4
Possible answers
Student exchanges, language learning, joint cultural events, and shared scientific and technological know-how can be carried out by individuals.

Trade agreements, transport links, and media images can be improved by governments.
Tourism can be carried out by both individuals and governments. Climate and landscape, and lifestyle and culture can be promoted by both as well.

5
a the overwhelming majority of people were in favour of
b with a smaller number naming lifestyle and food
c the most important languages after English by about equal numbers of people

6
a Sentence a relates to student exchanges, b relates to climate, and c relates to language learning.
b Sentence a is illustrated by pie chart 1, b could be illustrated by pie chart 2 or 4, and c is illustrated by pie chart 3.

7
a pie chart 1   b pie chart 3
c pie chart 1   d pie chart 2
e pie chart 4

8
a The vast majority of holiday makers to China …
b It is clear that almost equal numbers of both sexes …
c Only a tiny minority of filmgoers …
d In conclusion, the trend is clearly upward, with just under half of companies …
e To sum up, nearly a third of all tourists …

9

It is clear that	Overall
To conclude	It is evident that
It would seem that	In conclusion
To sum up	

Describing two sets of data

1
a Backpacking is popular with the youngest group and guided tours relatively unpopular. This pattern is reversed for the oldest group.
b 31–40 year olds   c satisfied

2
2 enjoyed   3 belong
4 accounts for   5 comes
6 make up   7 include
8 is rated

3
a As can be seen from the table
b the pattern
c These people make up 57 per cent of those on guided tours
d … with a massive 83 per cent from both groups stating they enjoyed their holiday

4
Students' own answers.

Using complex sentences: Concession (1)

1
a although, nevertheless
b *although* is a conjunction, *nevertheless* is an adverb. *Nevertheless* normally starts a sentence.
c but, however, despite
But is a conjunction, *however* is an adverb and normally comes near the beginning of a sentence. *Despite* can only be used before a noun or an *-ing* form.

2
a 3   b 1   c 5   d 2   e 4

3
a Although the vast majority of visitors to Britain come from Europe, they stay for fewer than ten days on average.
b Although 45 per cent of people speak a foreign language, the vast majority are at a low level.
c Despite its/the good weather, southern France is visited by only two per cent of Asian tourists.
d The number of student exchanges rose, but/although the cost of them went up.
e Although the event was promoted to teenagers, they accounted for only 32 per cent of the audience.

4
Students' own answers.

Task 2

Expressing advantages and disadvantages

1
Students' own answers.

2
a the first sentence
b the second sentence (advantages and disadvantages)

3

Some other entertainment devices may be possible.

a Advantage: MP3, DVD player
b Advantage: Mobile phone
c Disadvantage: MP3, handheld game
d Advantage: MP3, handheld game
e Advantage: MP3, mobile phone handheld game, DVD player
f Disadvantage: MP3
g Disadvantage: Mobile phone
h Disadvantage: MP3, handheld game

4

a benefits   b help
c difficult   d enable/help
e interfere   f ideal

5

Advantage: help, benefits, ideal, enable

Disadvantage: difficult, interfere, enable

6

a e
b for example, so, however, hence, nevertheless, because
c They help people to relax; they allow people greater freedom; they are a nuisance for other travellers.

7

1 for example   2 Even if
3 Likewise   4 though
5 Although   6 and
7 Consequently

8

a disadvantages
b b, c, d, e, f, h
c Main advantage: *this allows people greater freedom and flexibility and takes away the boredom of the journeys.*
Main disadvantage: *people are becoming more and more isolated in their own worlds. Consequently the art of communication is being lost.*

Using advantage and disadvantage vocabulary

1

a drawbacks   b chance
c gain   d problems
e handicap   f opportunities
g benefit

2

Serious emphasizes disadvantage.

3

Advantage: beneficial, useful, invaluable, helpful, convenient
Disadvantage: worthless, difficult

4

advantageous – disadvantageous
beneficial – detrimental
useful – useless
worthless – valuable/invaluable
invaluable – worthless
difficult – easy
helpful – unhelpful
convenient – inconvenient

5

Possible answers

a International arts festivals encourage interest in other people's cultures.
b Lending artworks to other countries improves their knowledge of other cultures.
c Films and concerts enhance the quality of people's lives.
d To enable children to value their heritage, we need to show them how strongly it still influences society today.
e Personal links can benefit travellers when they are out of their own country.
f Ignorance of other people's traditions can hinder business partnerships.
g To prevent countries falling out with each other, we need to promote interest in particular cultures.

Using complex sentences: Concession (2)

1

a 1 Although 2 Despite
b 2 emphasizes the advantage
  1 emphasizes the disadvantage

2

a Although
b However/Nevertheless
c Despite
d However/Nevertheless
e but

Unit 7

Task 1

Using adverbs

1

Students' own answers.

2

Students' own answers.

3

a There was little change over the period, only a slight increase from each source.
b The highest proportions were allocated by non-European countries (Japan and the USA).
c business
d the EU average
e The highest proportion was allocated by Japan, the lowest by Italy.

4

2 is shown   3 rose
4 came   5 contributed
6 overtook   7 was spent
8 contributed   9 was

5

slightly, approximately, consistently, closely, significantly, considerably

6

a significantly   b consistently
c highly   d slightly
e marginally   f considerably
g Approximately   h substantially

7

a 4 b 5 c 3 d 7 e 1 f 2 g 6

Using adverbs to evaluate data

1

It is also noticeable that
It is worth noting that

2

a Significantly, the number of scientists per head of population has declined in recent years.
b It is obvious that the sales failed to recover.
c Numbers will probably continue to fall over the period.
d It is clear that there were skill shortages in the chemical industry.
e It is evident that investment needs to be increased.
f It is noticeable that the pattern for investment in the arts is the reverse.
g It is important to note that the cost of plasma screens is set to fall.

3

Sentences b, c and d are possible.

4

a The number of science graduates fell significantly.

b Evidently, the number of technical staff in hospitals is falling.

c The cost of training scientists is increasing noticeably year by year.

d Investment in capital equipment like specialist machinery is down considerably on last year.

e Clearly, sales of new televisions soared before the World Cup.

f The trend is now obviously upward.

5

Possible answers

a Funding for R&D increased only marginally over the period.
Business provided approximately half of the investment in 2010.
The amount of funding increased very slowly over the period.

b Japan allocated considerably more of its national income to R&D than Italy.
Evidently, the four EU countries invested less than the USA or Japan.
The proportion of national income given to R&D was noticeably higher in Germany and France than in Italy.
The proportion allocated by the UK was only slightly above the EU average. Interestingly, the average proportion among EU countries was below that for Japan and the USA.

Avoiding irrelevance

1

a students on all courses at an Australian university

b seven

c maths

d physics, oriental languages

e chemistry

f Apparently not. For example, chemistry and physics are both science subjects but chemistry was seen as easy by 70 per cent of students and physics by only 25 per cent. Likewise, among language subjects, African languages were seen as easy by 60 per cent but oriental languages by only 20 per cent.

2

a irrelevant as it contains an unnecessary speculation

b relevant

c relevant

d irrelevant because it contains an unnecessary opinion

e relevant

f irrelevant as it gives too much data, or rather unnecessary information about how the bar chart is drawn

3

Possible answer

The bar chart shows whether students at an Australian university rated different subjects as easy, moderately difficult, or difficult.

The subject which was most commonly rated as difficult was maths, by 70 per cent of students. Only 20 per cent saw it as easy. Physics was also largely judged to be a difficult or moderately difficult subject. Only 25 per cent of students viewed it as easy. By contrast, chemistry was regarded as easy by a massive 70 per cent of students.

As far as language subjects are concerned, languages in general were seen as easy by 40 per cent of students. This percentage dropped to 20 per cent for oriental languages. African languages, however, were viewed as easy by 60 per cent of students. Art was judged to be an easy subject by only 30 per cent of students and, like physics, 50 per cent rated it as difficult.

In conclusion, there seems to be no clear correspondence between the type of subject and whether it was generally rated as easy or difficult.

Task 2

Discussing other people's opinions

1

a Frida Kahlo

b Stephen Hawking

2

Students' own answers.

Background information:

Leonardo da Vinci was a famous Italian artist and inventor who painted the Mona Lisa.

Albert Einstein was a famous

theoretical physicist who came up with the theory of relativity.

Sir Isaac Newton was an English scientist and mathematician who described the properties of gravity.

Nicolaus Copernicus was a Polish scientist who recognized that the Earth orbited the Sun.

3

a first sentence

b second sentence

c third sentence

4

1 c   2 b   3 a

5

Many people feel strongly; They argue; supporters of arts groups feel

6

a 4   b 1   c 3   d 5   e 2   f 8   g 7   h 6

7

Possible answers

b Some people feel that the wealth of a nation is connected with scientific development. They claim that modern economies cannot advance without a strong scientific base.

c A commonly held belief is that science is now playing a more important role in our lives than in the past. People feel that it has an effect on everything we do from eating to travelling.

d It is argued by some people that the work of artists should be censored. They maintain that certain works of art that are produced are offensive and should be banned.

e Some people think that scientists should have some involvement with artists, and vice versa. They believe that bringing these two groups together would be better for society as a whole.

f Some people feel that science is dull and boring. They maintain that spending time alone in laboratories without much human contact is not very interesting.

g It is argued by some people that many scientific experiments are dangerous to society. They claim that there are many examples where serious mistakes have been made.

h Yet others believe that the work of scientists should not be tightly regulated by society. They argue that by limiting scientific work, we might stop certain beneficial developments.

8

Possible answers

b A very good example here is Germany, which produces a large number of science graduates and has a thriving economy.

c For example, when we buy food from the supermarket the flavourings and additives have all been measured and tested scientifically.

d A case in point are certain works which depict religious figures.

e For instance, more regular contact between the two would help scientists to appreciate the way in which scientific advances are perceived in society as a whole.

f Take the job of lab technician, for example. It involves dealing with tests and test results, and there is very little human contact involved.

g A good example is certain tests in which possible new medical drugs were tried out on humans only to find that they had unforeseen and very serious effects on the subjects' health.

h For instance, how could we continue to research cures for diseases such as cancer or AIDS if the non-scientific community were allowed to interfere with scientists' work?

Hypothesizing

1

a 2 b 5 c 4 d 1 e 3

2

would, *could* and *might* talk about possibility.
Sentence d asks the reader to imagine a situation and its consequence.

3

a Unless they are encouraged by parents and teachers, aspiring musicians will not develop.

b If science stops the ageing process in humans one day, will this benefit mankind?

c Unless an effort is made to keep traditional farming methods alive, they will disappear.

d As long as innovation is encouraged, many new jobs will be created.

4

Possible answers

a Provided parents have an interest in music, they will encourage musical talent in their children.

b If government support for arts projects is not available, they will be forced to seek funding elsewhere.

c Unless entrance to museums and art galleries is free, many people will never experience them at all.

d Providing young scientists are given the right opportunities, the work they do has the potential to be of enormous benefit to society.

Unit 8

Making predictions

Task 1

1

Students' own answers.

2

Students' own answers.

3

a It shows predictions for the number of buildings that will be powered by solar and wind energy.

b They relate to the number of buildings.

c 0–600 million

4

a will

b predicted, will

c prediction, will

d predicted

5

a projection, forecast, anticipation

b projected, anticipated, forecast(ed)

c prediction: expectation, estimation
   predicted: expected, estimated, set

6

a is predicted, will provide

b are expected

c will come

d is forecast

e is not expected

f is projected, will be

g is set

h is anticipated, will provide

7

Sentence *a* describes something which will happen before a future time. Sentence *b* describes something in progress at a time in the future.

8

a will be using

b will have become

c will have been sold

d will be living

e will have been destroyed

9

Students' own answers.

Ensuring factual accuracy

1

a It is projected to increase.

b Ireland

c Hungary

d Yes, 64 per cent.

2

1 The charts show forecasts for the annual reforestation (*not deforestation*) rate in selected countries.

2 It is projected that Ireland will have the highest rate in 2030 at 1.7 per cent (*not 1.5 per cent*).

3 It is anticipated that the figure will rise more sharply to 1.1 per cent (*not 1.2 per cent*).

4 'very concerned' 25 per cent (*instead of 'not very concerned'*).

3

a It *is* predicted that the use of solar energy will become more important.

b We see from the chart that *the* largest amount of money was spent on the water conservation project.

c The chart shows the different types of trees *that/which* are found in different regions.

d From the pie chart, *it* can be seen that hydroelectric power constitutes seven per cent of the world energy demand.

e It is clear that *the* majority of people are very concerned about climate change.

f Recently a number of campaigns have encouraged people *to* plant trees.

4

a It *is* projected that Ireland will have the highest rate …

b … while at *the* same time there is a sizeable proportion of people who are not concerned.

Making predictions in the past

1

a It gives in thousands the estimated and actual numbers of houses built in the UK in 2010.

b seven

c below

d Southern England (77,500), London (47,800) and in Central England (16,200). These figures far exceeded the estimates.

e North of England. The estimate was 9,300 houses while the actual figure was 13,500.

f Northern Ireland and Wales. In Wales, it was estimated that 2,900 houses would be built, but the real figure was 6,300.
Likewise, in Northern Ireland the estimate was for 2,500 houses, but the real number was 5,000.

g Scotland.

h Scotland. It was estimated that 3,200 houses would be built but in the event the figure was only 3,000.

2

Possible answer

The diagram gives figures for the actual and estimated numbers of houses built in the UK by region in 2010.

In most cases, the estimated number was below the number of houses which were actually built. The highest numbers of houses were constructed in Southern England (77,500), London (47,800), and in Central England (16,200), far exceeding the estimates (51,100, 24,800 and 8,100 respectively). Similarly in the North of England, there was a disparity of just over 4,000 between the two figures, 9,300 houses for the estimated figure against 13,500 for the actual figure. Northern Ireland and Wales followed the same trend, 2,500 houses as opposed to 5,000, and 2,900 compared to 6,300. Scotland was the region where the lowest number of houses were built. It was

estimated that 3,200 houses would be constructed but in the event the figure was only 3,000.

In conclusion, it is clear that many more houses were built in the UK in 2010 than had been anticipated.

Task 2

Using articles

1

Students' own answers.

2

Possible answers

a The most serious threats are water shortages, drought and other natural disasters, as well as other effects of global warming.

b–d Students' own answers.

3

2 factories	3 pollutants
4 fish/wildlife	5 wildlife/fish
6 leisure	7 pressure
8 action	9 incentives

4

Countable: animal, tree, idea, situation, fact
Uncountable: information, nature, climate*, accommodation, knowledge, research, weather
climate can also be countable.

5

Countable: problem, factories, pollutants, incentives
Uncountable: wildlife, leisure, pressure, action
fish can be countable and uncountable.

6

a no article, no article

b no article

c the

d a, no article

e no article

f the

g The, no article

h The

7

a Wave power technology is the best answer to the problem of pollution. However, the introduction of such technology also creates *a* different problem.

b Governments worldwide should tax ~~the~~ cars more. A measure like this would make people think more about nature.

c In *the* near future, houses will be more energy-efficient than they are now.

d *The* food industry could pay for recycled bottles as was done in the past. The bottles would then not be thrown away.

e Insects like ~~the~~ bees, for example, play a vital role in most ecosystems. The bee pollinates plants and flowers.

f ~~The~~ Facilities like dams and forests are also used for leisure.

Writing conclusions

1

a 1 b 2 c 2 d 1 e 2 f 1 g 2

2

Question 1

Statement of most important measure: d

Another possible measure and why it is less effective: f

Restatement of most important measure and its consequences: a

Question 2

Statement of opinion: b

Reference to the opposite view: e

Reason against the opposite view: g

Restatement of opinion: c

3

In conclusion: to sum up, to conclude

I do not agree: I do not accept, I disagree with the idea that

All in all: in general, all things considered

I feel that: I believe, I would argue that

certainly: of course, no doubt

4

a There is no reason why local eco-friendly businesses cannot be successful.

b There is no reason why people could not take more holidays at home instead of always flying abroad.

c There is no reason why people could not travel by fast train instead of taking short flights.

d There is no reason why governments should not give special financial support to eco-friendly business people.

Unit 9

Task 1

Paraphrasing and using synonyms

1

Students' own answers.

2

Students' own answers.

3

a The graph gives information about the average use of beds in three typical hospitals around the world before and after day-surgery is introduced.

b While the trend was upward for the French hospital, the average bed occupancy dropped noticeably after the introduction of day-surgery.

c The trend for the Ukrainian hospital was similar to that of the French hospital, but the fall in bed use after 2009 was not as marked.

d You can make a connection between the coincidental fall in the budget for in-patient care and the fall in bed occupancy.

e You can use *trend* to summarize information.

You can use *upward* to show the direction of the trend.

You can use the phrase *similar pattern* to compare similarities.

You can use *reach a peak* to describe a high point.

You can use *except that* to introduce detail which is different from the general trend/pattern.

You can use *saw a continuous rise* as an alternative to *rose*.

You can use *change* to describe a difference that occurs.

You can use *coincide* to show when things happen at the same time, whether they are related or not.

4

2 impact	3 trend
4 occupancy	5 peak
6 falling	7 marked
8 experienced	9 rise
10 significantly	11 clear
12 reduction	

5

1 details – information
2 impact – effect
3 trend – tendency
4 occupancy – use
5 peak – high point
6 falling – dropping
7 marked – sharp
8 experienced – saw
9 rise – increase
10 significantly – considerably
11 clear – evident
12 reduction – cut/decrease

6

c 3   d 5   e 7   f 2   g 6   h 4

7

Incorrect answers to be deleted:
a says
b had an affect on
c reached a height
d design
e alternatively
f towards
g in contrast with
h can be viewed in

Checking spelling

1

a before	b receive
c studying	d useful
e personally	f sufficient
g definitely	h different
i choice	j referred

2

Spelling rules

Noun + *full*: remove the second *l* = *useful*.

Adverbs from adjectives ending in *-al*: add *-ly* and remove nothing, e.g. *personally*.

Adverbs from adjectives ending in *-e*: add *-ly* and keep the *e*, e.g. *definitely*.

Verbs ending with *y* + *-ing*: no change, e.g. *studying*.

Words of more than one syllable: the consonant doubles if the final syllable is stressed: *referred*.

3

a gradually
b which
c occurred
d peak
e figures, approximately
f fluctuated
g exceeded
h survey

4

average, accidents, dramatically, improvement, steadily, regards, motorcycle, occurring

Task 2

Using general nouns to link and summarize ideas

1

Students' own answers.

2

1 strangely	2 well
3 surprisingly	4 widely
5 accurately	6 often
7 seriously	8 well
9 frequently	10 Clearly

3

The paragraph follows sentence pattern a.

4

a information	b idea
c scheme	d measure
e issue	f solution
g knowledge	h opinion
i problem	

5

Possible answers

a This issue needs to be considered when planning the health care budget for any country.

b This idea could have benefits both for people's health and the education of doctors and nurses.

c This prediction may seem surprising, but I believe costs will be reduced as technology becomes more widely available.

d Initially, this may be a problem, but the changes will result in a more efficient health service.

e The situation, however, is one that can be prepared for by setting money aside for the future.

f Measures like this could lead to a significant improvement in the nation's health.

g Not surprisingly, it is a trend which is not looked on favourably by some western doctors.

h This is a matter that needs to be considered when planning for future spending.

Using cause and effect relationships

1

Possible answers

a music and health
Effect: helps people relax, takes up attention
Measure: music therapy, used sometimes to treat patients with communication problems

b alternative therapies and health
Example: homeopathy, herbalism
Information: contested by different people
Opinions: health practitioners versus people who have experienced these therapies
Effects: may be due to influence on the mind as well as body

c exercise and health
Effects: strengthens muscles, helps coordination, helps people to relax
Problem: high cost of gyms/health centres
Scheme: companies offer gym membership as part of package to staff

2

Students' own answers.

3

Students' own answers.

Ensuring verb-subject agreement

1

a is   b has   c are   d is
e has   f are   g is   h have

2

a This information is published all around us, even on cigarette packets.

b Unfortunately, this advice is not often followed.

c Instead, this work is carried out by health care assistants.

d Enormous progress has been made in understanding how disease spreads, …

e However, this equipment can be dangerous if it is not used properly.

f However, there is certainly some evidence that it can be beneficial.

g Some research has been carried out which shows that elderly people live longer if they live with a partner.

Unit 10

Task 1

Using the correct word order

1

Students' own answers.

2

Students' own answers.

3

a The chart refers to the main reasons for choosing a career according to age group.

b They refer to the reasons under consideration.

c The most noticeable features are the importance of money and the position of friends.

d The most noticeable features are the importance of money and parents.

e The younger age group put money first; the older age group put parents first.

4

1 the main reasons for choosing a career

2 were influenced by the various factors

3 were the reverse for the 40–50 age group

4 As regards teachers and role models

5 nine and fifteen per cent respectively for the younger group

6 The only similarity between the two age groups

7 than any other factors

5

a The sales of *specialist* tours have fallen recently.

d It is clear that the number of flats *occupied* by single people in major cities in the West is putting pressure on housing.

e From the graphs, it can be concluded that young people *are* much more mobile than previous generations.

f The pursuit of a professional career among both men and women has led to a *noticeable* reduction in the birth rate.

g There are *several* similarities in the presentation of the data.

h Overall, the chart shows that the media are responsible for turning *people* into celebrities.

Linking information and data using *with*

1

a an explanation

b *with* is normally followed by a noun then a verb in the *-ing* form.

2

a Sales were upward for most of the year, with profit reaching a peak in December.

b The main reason for career choice was ambition, with 50 per cent choosing it.

c It is expected that the price of one-bedroom flats will rise, with accommodation for individuals being in short supply.

d The pattern was different, with passenger numbers dropping in summer and rising in winter.

e The trend was clearly upward, with manufacturing costs decreasing at the same time.

f Consumption of energy rose, with the highest point being in January.

Task 1 revision

1

a True   b False   c False   d False
e True   f False   g False   h True

Task 2

Using the appropriate paragraph structure

1

Question 1: b, a, c
Question 2: b, d, a, c
Question 3: c, d, b, a

2

Question 1: a
Question 2: c
Question 3: b

3

Possible answers

Money does not make happiness. To what extent do you agree or disagree?

It is impossible to deny that money helps people to achieve happiness because it is extremely hard to do anything in life without it. For example, if you want to see a film or a play at the theatre, you need money for the ticket and for transport. Also, if you want to have a relaxing time at home you still need money, even to buy a TV or a computer. (structure b)

It is better to reform criminals instead of just punishing them. What measures could be taken to attempt to integrate law-breakers back into society?

Personally, I think that criminals of all levels should be given a chance to be a part of society rather than just being put into prison. If this is done, then the offender will have a better chance of not reoffending. Society will also not have to pay for the cost of keeping criminals in prisons, which are very expensive places to run. Of course, then society as a whole will benefit. (structure c)

Distinguishing between relevant and irrelevant information

1
Text 1
1 b   2 a   3 a
Text 2
4 a   5 b   6 b
Text 3
7 a   8 b

2
Students' own answers.

Task 2 revision

1
If you want to achieve a good score band, you need to be able to tick all of the items in the list.

2
Possible answers
a for example, for instance, a case in point is, like
b because, as, one reason for this is, since
c as a result, therefore, so, this means that, this leads to
d moreover, furthermore, in addition, and, also
e if, unless, provided
f but, however, while, whereas, despite
g although, despite
h and so, and therefore, to sum up, all in all, in general

3
Possible answers
a Problem and solution
b Measures and results
c Cause and effect
d Reason and example
e Example and specific example
f Effect and example
g Additional information and example
h Condition/Hypothesis and result
i Concession and contrast

4
Possible answers
a Money is not as important as friends, because it cannot provide emotional support.
b For many people, keeping fit and healthy is the main factor which is necessary for a good quality of life. However, developing a healthy mind is just as important.
c If one is content with life, then there is no longer any need to pursue unrealistic ambitions.
d What is involved in achieving a good quality of life depends on many factors rather than just one. For example, money is important to gain a certain financial security, but it is not enough on its own.
e Happiness and contentment are more important than the pursuit of freedom. The latter aim is an illusion as nobody is ever completely free.
f Many people living in poor housing conditions are still happy. So the idea that you have to have a high standard of living to be happy is false.

5
Possible answers
Other people believe that the family plays an important role in maintaining a good quality of life. You just have to look at societies where there are extended families to see how much more content people are because they are surrounded by relatives who love them and can look after them if they fall ill or have problems. This support is not just financial but also emotional.